MY

MW01706268

SELVES

A MEMOIR

with best wishes,
Morris Schnitzer

MORRIS SCHNITZER

LUGUS

MY THREE SELVES
Morris Schnitzer

Canadian Cataloguing in Publication Data

ISBN: 1-896266-60-6

Published by:

LUGUS PUBLICATIONS
48 Falcon Street
Toronto, ON M4S 2P5
Canada

416 322 5113 (Voice)
416 484 9512 (Fax)

© Morris Schnitzer, 2002

This book is not to be copied in any form whatsoever without the written permission of the Publisher.

The Publisher acknowledges the assistance of Mr. Robert Greenberg, The Vered family, Mr. Mendel Good and The Canadian Jewish Congress in the publication of this book.

To my parents and my brother Benno
who perished in the Holocaust.

CONTENTS

FOREWORD

I grew up with my father's stories of his childhood in Germany and his lost youth during the war. Thanks to these stories and the success I knew he had made of himself since then, I grew up with a strong belief in the human spirit as well as a strong connection with other horror stories we hear all the time. I can't be sure of all the lessons my father expected me to draw from his stories; I'm sure he knew I'd draw my own no matter what he intended, and so will you. And you will laugh, you will cry, you will rage, you will be on the edge of your chair. These are the stories of a determined survivor, a kid who beat the Orwellian, Nazi system time and time again—barely, but he did it and he came out whole.

What I would like you to keep in mind as you read this book is that the young man who emerged from this maelstrom had somehow managed to hold on to not only his physical self and his intelligence but also his essential humanity. He was not bitter, not twisted into hatred by his experiences; he might be aghast, woeful, outraged, contemptuous. He blamed the people who did nothing, who went along, who betrayed, who took part; there was never any excuse for selling your soul, for losing your humanity. And he could even laugh at the stupidity of the SS, tripping over their own overly-polished boots, seeing nothing but their own obsessions. Ah, he was the greatest fan of "Hogan's Heroes" later in life!

He knew he was no superhero, either, nor blessed nor chosen. But I think he was—and is, at 80 summers now—particularly gifted. Yes, he had the benefit of an old-fashioned, well-rounded, bourgeois German-Jewish education but, I think, he had a variety of talents he was fortunate enough to be able to mine from an early age.

He and his brothers studied several languages, went to the schools best suited to each one, learned to argue at the dinner table, travelled round Germany, knew people from different backgrounds and social classes, played lots of football, learned to defend themselves—in short, they became confident, flexible, fairly sophisticated and tough for their ages. The latter was my father's biggest hurdle from the first day he found himself working on a farm in northern Holland; it was Berlin boy meets the Spartans. His misadventures in ice-cold, Frisian ditches at dawn or with ice-cold, Frisian farmers could make me weep with laughter. In fact, there was often some comic relief in the way he talked about his physical hardships, his encounters with authorities or his narrow escapes. I always thought his ability to keep on seeing the absurdity, the upside-down madness of his situation, kept him going as much as did his recognition of the everyday realities to be faced. Somewhere in his mind, no matter what role or what situation he was in at the time, there was always the original Moritz Schnitzer, not only monitoring his performance but also standing outside the madness—at least, I believe there must have been because, somehow, he emerged intact.

He had another significant advantage, one which he always stressed to me: the final conversation with his father in Bochum after the events following *Kristallnacht*, just before leaving home on the *kindertransport* for Holland. I won't spoil the story for you. Suffice it to say that this is one of those instances of fateful timing, one of those moments of pure luck of which my father insists he had many. The message his father, Hermann, gave him in that short meeting was vital; it made his path clear and his mind determined. Of course, by that time they had all been living with the Nazis for some years and could no longer underestimate their fanaticism, but Hermann's words were really my father's final solution, in the best sense of the phrase.

I must mention my murdered, lost family: my grandparents, Hermann and Rosa, and my redheaded uncle, Benno. When I first got to know them, in my childhood, I wanted to know what they were like, I tried most of all to bring them to life in my mind, through my father's anecdotes and descriptions. It was only much later, in my thirties, with a redheaded son of my own, that I would be suddenly and repeatedly overwhelmed by grief. The thought of those parents, dignified and hard-working people who had once believed they lived in the greatest country in the world, herded into ghettoes and then cattle cars and then death camps with their youngest son...the thought of Benno, a teenage boy seeing his world collapse into madness, barely having lived any happy moments in his short time...and my grandmother, who hadn't been able to part with him, how she must have suffered as she saw his life slowly strangled away.

At last I was able to put myself in their place, and to miss them. What surprises me most when I look back at myself growing up with these constant reminders of the depths of human depravity is that I was never frightened of the world, I was never made to feel that I too would be hunted down one day. Rather I was learning to take the signs more seriously than did my grandparents, and thus prevent such things happening again. It was all in the way of telling, it was all so measured and, with the benefit of hindsight, we could see the escalation of events. I learned the simple fact that even in the most so-called civilized of societies, circumstances can turn sour and be exploited by powermongers and madmen, and ordinary people can turn against each other thinking, who knows, that they have something to gain. I learned that yes, the truth is that, in order to protect ourselves and safeguard our rights to our beliefs and practices, we must stand by everyone else's rights as well. There is no way out of it; we are condemned to coexist; we are interdependent; fair is fair, and all that. We must look out for each other. I learned that we must be vigilant, not let our own prejudices go unanalyzed or others' unanswered. Yes, it can happen here as it can happen anywhere but it's not going to if we can remain vigilant. This book is one more small contribution to that struggle.

Since those early years, I've lived in different places and in recent years I've been teaching immigrants to Canada, many of them members of persecuted minorities like my father. Most of them are also similar to him in that they are well-educated and well-rounded and also, very ambitious, as he was when he finally managed to get to Canada and study. Often they have that wry sense of humor that has helped keep them going, too. Occasionally they have told me stories of their own that I've rushed to tell to my father, to unburden myself to someone who knows and to let him know that I continue to be aware of the whole spectrum of human possibilities. And I tell my students, those new storytellers, that we must all make the best of what we have here and never be led into that downward spiral from prejudice to persecution. But in fact, they tend to know that better than most Canadians, I find.

So read this book, too, as one of many refugee stories. Like so many others, it can be hard to take, I admit. But read it and count yourself lucky that you can afford to sit back and contemplate the human condition, that you can live these hard lessons secondhand. Read it and find yourself slowly but surely enmeshed in one of the darkest periods of history, when there were factories of death in the middle of Europe. Read it and rejoice in getting away with your life again and again, for you will survive and you will not even enter one of those death camps with my father. This book will make you proud to be human as well as ashamed. It will remind you of how people both betrayed and defended their essential humanity in a time so close to our own and in places supposedly so much like our own. It will bring you closer to the nightly news on television, where you can always find stories like these. It will give you an example of incredible levelheadedness, ingenuity, determination and integrity. It will, I hope, put your own life into perspective for some time to come.

Eve Schnitzer
Ottawa, Canada
September, 2002

Acknowledgments

The author thanks his late wife, Leah, for insisting that he write this memoir and for transcribing the first draft; his daughter, Eve, for organizing the manuscript in its present form and for her Foreword; Seymour Mayne, distinguished Canadian poet, and his wife, Sharon Katz, for long-term encouragement and active assistance with the publication of this book.

CHAPTER I
THE FAMILY, THE SETTING

I was born into a Jewish family in Germany in 1922. The old city of Bochum, Westphalia, some forty kilometres east of the Rhine, was (and is) one of the industrial centres of the Ruhr Valley. Then as now, the Ruhr Basin had the biggest steel mills in Germany. Steelworks ranged along roadsides in Bochum near the coalmines which fed the coke-ovens. A mere ten kilometres from us loomed Essen, one of the major industrial cities of Europe, with the enormous iron and steel making plants founded by the Krupp family in the early 19th century.

My father was Hermann Schnitzer. He had immigrated to Germany in 1908 from Galizia in what was to become Poland. At that time it was part of the Austro-Hungarian Empire. In those days Europe was a very different place in many ways. My father was only about fourteen years old, just past his *bar mitzvah* when he left home on his own.

He started out buying and selling farm produce in Germany. Like many Jewish migrants in different corners of the world throughout history, he began as a travelling pedlar. Then, at the age of sixteen, once he knew the ropes and had the contacts, he decided to become an egg wholesaler. But, even then, a license was required to sell almost anything in Germany. When my father applied to the bureau and was asked his age, he was told he was too young to be granted a license.

But he acquired his documentation somehow and launched a wholesale business. He was successful from the start. He had exceptional business ability.

His father had re-located in Germany before him, but was never successful there. Maybe he just couldn't adjust to the conditions or to the language; life was very different in his native Galizia where he had spoken Yiddish, and he had also left as an older man.

My father adapted readily and did well. His two older brothers, Beryl and Josef, followed him to Germany. Then he brought his sisters, Rosa and Augusta, there. Finally, in 1922 after I was born, he brought his youngest brother, Mischel. But my father's mother never left Poland.

During the 1914-1918 war, my father enlisted in the army. Austria and Germany were allies and, as an Austrian citizen, he served with German troops in the infantry corps. He fought in several battles on the eastern front and was decorated with the Iron Cross.

He was taken prisoner in Russia and confined to work in the forests—he was soon in charge of a timberyard: even as a prisoner of war my father used his talent for management.

After the war he settled back in Germany, land of opportunity. Then in 1921 he made a trip to the place of his birth, a town called Rozniatov. It is in the Carpathian foothills near Stanislav, not far from Czernowitz. He married my mother there and whisked her off to Germany, where she too was to flourish in a more challenging and rewarding world. My mother, as an only child, refused to leave her mother behind, so they took her with them. My grandmother was also to prove a great support for us all.

My mother's family name was Heller. 'Berta' was what my father called her although her given name was Rosa and her Hebrew name was Miriam. She was the daughter of Moishe Heller, a well-to-do man who died in 1908. He was supervising the construction of a building when a wall collapsed on him, crushing his kidneys. He went for treatment to a hospital in Vienna, the leading medical centre of the world at that time. The most able doctors tried to save him but couldn't. He was buried in the *Zentrale Friedhof* (Central Cemetery) there. In 1932 my mother journeyed to Vienna to oversee the erection of a headstone on his gravesite.

After his death my grandmother managed their hardware store in Rozniatov. It was the only establishment of its kind in that sprawling countryside and it prospered. However, once my parents were married and my grandmother was gone the store closed.

In 1922, when I was born, my father owned a chain of retail shops in the Ruhr. Three of the shops were in Wattenscheid, a town situated about six kilometres from Bochum. When I was six weeks old, my parents moved there. Today Wattenscheid no longer exists as a separate entity; it has been absorbed by Bochum.

My father's shops specialized in household furnishings, boots and shoes, and every conceivable article of clothing. Both my parents worked in the clothing store in Wattenscheid, which was in the same building as our home. My mother had grown up in a retail business and was a super saleswoman. Often when I was in the store a customer would come in to buy a single item like a pair of pants. She would sell him a three-piece suit, a shirt and tie and a hat. He would spend more than he had originally intended but he would leave the store satisfied!

Besides me, our family included two younger brothers, Edmund and Benno. Eddi was born in 1923 and Benno in 1925. We were all raised by our maternal grandmother, Baba Shoshi, who took charge of the children and the housekeeping. A young live-in maid helped her.

Baba Shoshi was descended from a line of rabbinical scholars and her chief concern was our Jewish education. She was very religious: she prayed many times each day and I copied her; I did what she did. From the age of three I could recite or read Hebrew prayers fluently. Learning from her example, I was well advanced in reciting the liturgy.

Wattenscheid was then a town of sixty thousand people, a highly industrial area with coal mines all around. Every day we saw miners going to work with lamps in their helmets. From our home we could see them descending into the pits.

Most of our customers were miners. Early on, we became well acquainted and I knew the hazards they faced. They put in long hours of dirty, back-breaking work in narrow, damp, dark suffocating passageways. Their lives were always in danger.

Some of the region's miners were Polish in origin and had Polish names; many were Germans; the population was mixed. Even the immigrants from Poland had been in Germany for some time; few spoke Polish.

Coal mining was the main industry of Wattenscheid. I went to school with the children of miners, steelworkers, business and professional people. Of sixty thousand residents, about a hundred were Jews. That is to say, only twenty-five to thirty Jewish families lived in Wattenscheid.

The Wassermanns were our closest Jewish friends. They lived three or four blocks from us. The Spiegels lived a ten-minute walk away. There was no ghetto, and no segregation of Jews.

Our furniture store was located on the *Hochstrasse* (High Street) in the upper town. Our shoe and general clothing stores stood in the main business district downtown, at opposite ends of *Oststrasse*. There were two large apartments over the general store. We lived in one of them.

Our immediate neighbors were all non-Jews. The pharmacy across from our house belonged to the pharmacist Schulte, a wealthy and nationalistic German who lived there with his family. He had several sons, all of whom were older than me. I grew up with them. Their mother was a haughty woman whose family owned much of the land in Wattenscheid.

All of our friends and neighbors lived above their stores; this was common at the time. There were no poor people in our neighborhood: all were business or professional people of substantial means.

This part of Germany was prosperous: it was industrialized, dynamic, and people earned relatively high wages. I am sure that my father had chosen to live there because the area favored enterprise—and hard work.

CHAPTER II
CHILDHOOD MEMORIES

In 1927, when I was five, Eddi was four, and Benno just a toddler of two, my parents decided to show us the place where they had come from. The whole family, including Baba Shoshi, travelled first-class by train and spent two months in Poland.

I remember Baba Shoshi's house in Rozniatov. It was a beautiful stone building several storeys high, with a large hardware store on the ground floor. It was a strange place. Goods were still on the shelves although the store had been closed for years, since my parents' wedding.

During our stay my father rented a horse-drawn carriage and hired a driver. We drove around from village to village through the rolling rural landscape, with well-kept farms, and forests with lots of creatures in the wild. There were very few bridges, so often the horses plunged into shallow rivers and streams to cross. We were thrilled by this each time; we had never experienced anything like it in Germany!

Wherever we went, it seemed to me that my father was received like royalty. Maybe it was partly small-town hospitality, and partly the predictable welcome for a returning prodigal son. But my father, who—to his credit and his misfortune—was never one to be tight with money, also made bountiful donations to every local synagogue and institution. His ties to the area were strong: his mother was still living there with his sister Dina, whose husband had decamped to Brazil by himself in 1922. My father was the sole support of his mother for many years, and of Dina and her three children until 1935. Then my Aunt Dina and three cousins also emigrated to Brazil. My father sent money to his mother every month no matter what the circumstances. She was one of his prime concerns. His brothers and sisters, apparently, never helped to maintain her. Sometimes my parents had heated arguments over this.

I suppose my father was an idealist; an idealist and, in the final analysis, a dreamer. But his idealism made a deep impression on me, and it stayed alive in me even when it became tempered with the most bitter doses of reality. He was active in the Socialist Party in Germany and had many friends who were involved in politics. He was also a dedicated Zionist. Whenever world Zionist leaders would visit our region, my father met them personally and helped organize their rallies. Not only was he generous in contributing time, energy and money toward Israel, but he also hoped to settle there. Often he spoke of wanting us to grow up as Jews in *Eretz Yisrael.*

He was ready to move to what was then Palestine, in 1928. We children were all preschoolers; he was thirty-four years old. At that stage in his life, with a firm financial base, he felt able to pull up roots and branch out in new directions.

It was my mother who balked at going. She was very fond of Germany, probably then the most advanced country in the world. She enjoyed German cultural life and wanted her children to have the benefits of German culture and education. All in all, she refused to uproot herself and us for a barren, undeveloped place like Palestine. And so we stayed. The road to hell is paved with good intentions...

I began to attend school in 1928, when I was six years old. In fact, I had tried to go to school once before, to the only local preschool, which was run by Catholics. I had had a nice morning there but when my grandmother picked me up, she asked me what I had been learning. When I told her we had been singing songs about Jesus, she decided I wouldn't be going back there and continued to teach me herself at home. But now that I was of school age, there was more choice. Most schools in our region belonged to one of three systems: Catholic, Protestant, or 'Free' schools.

In the Ruhr Valley, Socialists were politically powerful. They ran their own schools, free of religious instruction. The *Freie Schule* in Wattenscheid was called the *Lessing Schule*, in honor of the great and tolerant eighteenth-century German writer, Gotthold Ephraim Lessing. I was a pupil at the *Lessing Schule*, and the only Jewish boy in the class.

The school was in the upper town. The Catholic school was close by. I had to pass by the Catholic school to get to school and to return home. And that is where I endured my first ordeal.

When I was on my way home from school, each and every day, three or four Catholic boys would be waiting for me. They would jeer at me with words like: *Jude Itzig Nase Spitzig!* which was a well-known rhyme among Germans. It meant: "Jew by the name of Izzie with a sharp nose."

They beat me up and pelted me with stones. Every time it was like running the gauntlet. I was alone, while they were always in packs. No classmate ever rallied to help me. Grownups would hurry by seemingly not realizing what was going on.

A number of times I took refuge in our furniture store, where my Uncle Mischel was manager. I would scuttle inside and pour out to him what was happening. Then he would take me home.

So my father supplied me with an escort. One of our office staff was assigned to convey me to and from school every day.

Sometimes my brothers and I were stoned by other kids, when we went out. We learned to stroll in groups. Then, one day, when they attacked us, we threw stones back, returned the blows, and scared them off.

These incidents occurred in 1928 when I was in first grade. They stopped after that, probably because we fought back!

Throughout my early school years I was aware of social unrest and business setbacks around me. There were business failures accompanied by increasing unemployment in 1928. Since my father was advancing merchandise on credit to scores of Jewish pedlars from Poland, he lost ruinous sums of money at that time. I could hardly avoid overhearing the quarrels in my house.

The pedlars used to throng our stores every morning, replenishing their stock of goods. Then they would fan out to sell in the region. My father expected these men to pay him for the stock they took, but some of them never did. My parents had formidable arguments about it. My mother would say my father was gullible and trusted people too much. His position was that he was right to trust people.

In 1929 circumstances started to deteriorate. By 1931-32 most of the pedlars were unable to pay anything because their customers were short of cash. It was the depth of the Depression and my father was teetering on the verge of bankruptcy.

Then my mother prevailed on him to keep out of the stores. He withdrew to a mountain resort in the Black Forest while she set to work. She collected some outstanding debts and reduced the army of pedlars, pared unprofitable goods and services and succeeded in saving the business.

My father was an expansive and impressive personality. He conceived vast schemes and dreams. He had fulfilled these ideas in part, but the times were no longer for dreamers.

By contrast, my mother was a pragmatic, down-to-earth person. She never labored under illusions. She was a doer who set herself limited aims and accomplished them efficiently.

Her mother, Baba Shoshi, lived with us until I was ten years old. Often she would murmur that she hated Germany. "Germans are vulgar," she would complain. Then suddenly one day in 1932 she announced that she was going back to Poland. Soon afterward, she kissed us goodbye. Not long after, we learned that she was ill with cancer. She had gone back to Poland to die.

She had sometimes spoken of being buried in Poland. When we heard of her illness, my father went to spend some time with her. A few months later she was dead, and I was heartbroken.

But life went on, and even in sad and uncertain times our family managed to take holidays away from sooty Wattenscheid. My parents usually took vacations separately so that one of them could stay behind to run the stores. Their choice of holiday spots differed: my father preferred to slow down and rest in a quiet environment while my mother loved the whirl of elegant spas.

I often tagged along with my mother. She tolerated this because I was obedient and well-behaved—the typical, serious, eldest son. Eddi, on the other hand, was inclined to tear around wildly, breaking glasses and creating havoc. And Benno was simply too small to be taken along.

I loved the setting of the spas. The buildings were usually white or pastel-colored. The parks were green and fresh, with flowered promenades and clear rivers. It was a blissful change from our coal-black region and I have always remembered these places with fondness.

There were outdoor concerts and theatrical shows. The tea-dances were intriguing. What I loathed was drinking medicinal waters: my mother believed these could benefit a variety of ailments. And I disliked having to lie down to rest for two hours after lunch.

Nonetheless, I thrived on the attention of the men, who played chess with me, and the women, who pinched my cheeks and tried to fatten me up with rich pastries or berries smothered in whipped cream. My mother and the other ladies continually worried that I was too thin and acted as if they had to rescue me from starvation. I suppose I was a rather bony child, and with my thatch of platinum-blond hair I was nicknamed *Der Alte* (the Old One) by my classmates. Certainly, my serious demeanor and my years with Baba Shoshi had made it easy for me to sit for hours with adults.

I visited a famous resort in Poland with my mother in 1932. Called Zakopane, it lies in the Carpathian Mountains near Cracow. It floats in my memory like a dream, and I no longer feel sure I could describe faithfully what it was really like.

In 1933 or 1934 our whole family took a cruise down the Rhine River. We saw the castles and crags of German legends. It was a lovely way to travel. On other occasions I accompanied my mother to German resorts such as her favorite, Bad Ems, or Bad Kreuznach, Bad Neuenahr, Bad Soden, or Baden-Baden.

CHAPTER III
GROWING UP, 1932-33

Of course school continued to intrude between holidays! Primary school in Germany lasted four years. In 1932 I completed this level and began Gymnasium, which was then the classical secondary school for boys.

The Gymnasium building was closer to our home than the *Freie Schule* had been. I was friendly with many of my non-Jewish classmates: we played soccer together and frequently visited each others' homes. Robert Schulte, the pharmacist's son, was a few years older than I was. I saw him at school every day and sometimes we walked there or back together.

Most of my Jewish education was acquired at home from private teachers. As far back as I remember, my brothers and I were taught both Hebrew and Talmud—the oral law and commentaries on the Torah. Teachers were engaged at considerable expense to instruct us for a few hours two afternoons a week. Since our own Jewish community was so small, they had to come to our house from Essen, a train journey that took an hour each way. So their entire afternoon was used up.

When I was ten years old, in the same year I began Gymnasium, my father decided that my brothers and I should learn English. From then on we took private English lessons regularly. I don't know just what possessed him; certainly it was not yet a common opinion that English would be a major language of the future. Looking back, I suppose he knew we youngsters would leave Germany one day. English was, after all, not only the language of the United States, where so many immigrants went, but it was also still the language spoken in Palestine under the British Mandate. Whatever his reasons were, he did a great service for me and for Eddie by forcing us to learn English from a young age. My English was to serve me well long before I got to Canada.

In fact we had quite a barrage of languages, although at the time we didn't appreciate it. At home we spoke Yiddish and German. At school, while I was starting English at home, I had Latin from the first year of Gymnasium. In third year, when I was thirteen, I also had French, and in fourth year, English. By that time my English was relatively well advanced, which was lucky for me because the method of teaching was to plunge us into the classics—like Sir Walter Scott, who haunts me to this day—using translation and grammatical explanations to get us out of a sea of foreign words. I suspect I was one of the few who could follow the lessons!

And then, of course, there were those eternal Hebrew and Talmud lessons. We were extremely busy. I remember one teacher who came to our house on Sunday afternoons: as soon as we saw him approaching, we would run off to the soccer game! The hapless man had to wait around until we slipped back home.

But we had outstanding teachers. One was a Mr. Gershenovitz, who taught us modern Hebrew; he had studied for his doctorate in Tübingen under the renowned Professor Kittel. Another was a Mr. Weissmann, who taught us modern Hebrew and *Tanach-Torah*, Prophets and other writings.

Our first English teacher was the daughter of Mr. Oppenheim, the cantor of the Wattenscheid congregation. She had a doctorate in pedagogy and had specialized in English. She was a professor of linguistics and a brilliant teacher. I believe that she emigrated to South Africa, so perhaps she was one who survived the looming genocide...

There were other lessons, besides. For a number of years I studied violin; I played quite well but wasn't keen on practising. Eddie drew very well and took lessons in sketching from an established artist. My father spent a fortune on our education; there was no limit to it. He had infinite respect for learning. And he knew it was something we could carry with us wherever we might go.

It was a nervous political period in 1932 when I started at the Gymnasium. There were six million unemployed in Germany. Our region was hit very hard.

The Communists were strong in our area and the Socialists, too, had large segments of the population behind them. The Nazis were gaining in strength and were even more militant than the Communists: they were fighting in the open—strutting about and beating up people in the streets.

We weren't alarmed by the Nazis because they weren't in power. They seemed to us more like rowdies and ruffians than a menace to the state. At least, this was the picture I got from my parents and other adults around me whenever they discussed politics. I used to listen to the radio and I heard Hitler's shrill harangues. Little by little, I picked up what the political parties were all about.

There was tremendous agitation and huge political rallies. Everyone anticipated a major event. No-one knew what was going to happen because the economic situation was so desperate. My parents talked about politics endlessly; in fact, it seemed they never talked about anything else.

Before the elections that gained the Nazi Party the largest number of seats, we thought that Hitler would never win. We believed there would be too much opposition to him, that the other parties would stymie his moves.

In fact, just the opposite happened. The right-wing and nationalist parties which leaned toward the centre regarded the Communists as their main opposition. Actually many people, at least in our area, expected the Communists to win. So, following the elections in July and November of 1932 when both the Nazi and the Communist parties attracted strong support, Hitler skilfully used the fear of Communism to swing the moderate parties behind him. By manipulating the Red Scare, he managed to attain power with support from the moderates.

I remember my father's prognostications. "If Hitler gains power, he won't last more than six months. Hitler doesn't know economics. He can't run Germany without knowing economics. He can't run a complex government in a modern society."

The election returns were close. In our region the Nazi Party wasn't strong but that didn't make any difference. After a series of weak short-lived governments, Hitler was asked to become Chancellor at the end of January, 1933. My parents were stunned; they couldn't imagine what the next step would be. They knew Hitler's political and social philosophy but didn't take him seriously: my father described him as an adventurer who couldn't hold things together; he thought the economy under Hitler would collapse before long.

My father misjudged Hitler completely, as of course did many others inside and outside Germany. People deluded themselves: they thought Hitler could be controlled, or they brushed him off as a temporary aberration that would soon disappear. And they were so mournfully wrong. Hitler dominated everyone around him. Using surprise, propaganda and repressive tactics, he lasted much longer and did indescribably more harm than was ever predicted.

Within a year of taking office, Hitler had eliminated all the other political parties. Germany was a one-party state. Hitler forced everyone to fall in line or risk severe penalties or death.

My Uncle Josef was a bellwether in 1933. He owned a fashionable shoe store in Bochum. The store was favorably located and, whenever I was there, it was crowded with customers. It was a gold mine, according to my father.

Shortly after the Nazi Party assumed power, Uncle Josef was savagely beaten. His skin turned completely blue. The assailants warned him to clear out of Bochum. Then a foreign newspaper printed a picture of him to illustrate Nazi brutality.

He was hospitalized for two weeks. When he was discharged, he came to our house to hide. For six weeks he was holed up in a small room in the attic: he was terrified of being found and too scared to return to Bochum. Since his picture had been published abroad, he was afraid of being beaten again or killed.

We never knew why he was attacked. My parents immediately assumed that it was a personal attack and not an assault against Jews: such was their faith in German civilization. I think now that his business success aroused some poisonous envy and made him an early victim. He was certainly not a Communist; on the contrary, he was an outright capitalist.

Around that time, the principal of the *Freie Schule* in Wattenscheid, an admirable man called Rector Mank who was a true democrat and a pacifist, was summarily exiled by the Nazis to a one-room school in a remote part of Germany. Rumors of other attacks and demotions circulated, and many reports of these appeared in the newspapers abroad. But Uncle Josef was the only Jew we knew to whom this sort of thing had happened. My parents shrugged it off. "This isn't the end of the world," they said. "Maybe he did some harm to someone and that person took revenge."

But after that, Uncle Josef was afraid to stay in Germany. He sold his business and moved to Palestine. There were no currency restrictions yet, so he took any money he had with him. He left Germany with his family in 1933.

Unemployment went down swiftly after Hitler rose to power. He built armaments and prepared for war. The economy recovered in a phenomenal way. Our stores were crowded from morning till evening; we could barely handle the volume.

The next disturbing incidents took place at the Gymnasium as students began joining the Hitler Youth. Soon they were wearing the brown shirt, black pants and big belt to school. Teachers also joined the Nazi Party. *Die Fahne Hoch*, *Horst Wessel*, and other songs were sung at class meetings.

Eventually I was the only one in the class who didn't belong to the Hitler Youth. I was the only Jewish boy in my class. Often all the other students wore their uniforms and so I rather stood out—a visible minority of one.

The odd thing is that, though they belonged to the Hitler Youth, many classmates were still my friends. Most of them didn't stop talking to me. It was like the Boy Scouts at first; they joined that club and I didn't. All of them knew I was Jewish, yet they didn't ostracize me. In the early years I felt but slight discomfort. But the strain increased inexorably as time went on.

CHAPTER IV
GROWING UP, 1933-37

Until 1933 there was little cohesion among Jews in Wattenscheid. My father, for one, had a low opinion of services at the local synagogue. Every year on High Holidays, on *Rosh Hashanah* and *Yom Kippur*, our family used to walk to and from the synagogue in Gelsenkirchen, four kilometres each way.

After 1933, though, the Jewish community in Wattenscheid began to gel. Jews were excluded from clubs and activities so we created structures in a centre of our own. A varied and active community life developed for those few remaining years.

Every Friday night and Saturday all the young people flocked to the synagogue. When my brothers and I became involved, our parents were drawn in too. My father joined us regularly: before he had seldom gone to synagogue. He wasn't a religious man. He came with us because he felt he should.

It was remarkable to see all the Jews in synagogue. We never lacked a *minyan*, or quorum; until then such participation had been impossible. People drew together as the larger community pushed them out. Now synagogue became the pivot of our lives.

Wattenscheid was too small to have a rabbi of its own. Instead we had a cantor who also acted as rabbi and gave sermons. Actually, Cantor Oppenheim's main occupation was that of teacher in the *Freie Schule*. He had been my class teacher in 1932, in my final year there, and his daughter had been our English tutor.

Long established though small, the synagogue was furnished with simple benches. Women sat in the balcony and men on the main floor. A short distance away was the *Gemeindehaus* or community centre, where Cantor Oppenheim lived in rooms upstairs. Downstairs there were meeting rooms and games rooms with ping-pong tables and chess, checkers and card tables. We organized frequent events and many Zionist activities. Every Saturday afternoon we held an *Oneg Shabbat* or sabbath celebration, where Cantor Oppenheim told rabbinic stories and we sang Hebrew songs.

The cantor trained all the young men to *daven*, or pray: he taught us to read the Torah with *neginot*, with the proper liturgical chant and traditional melodies. He instructed us in how to perform as *chazan*, or cantor, and how to lead prayers. He gave us repeated opportunities to practise: on Friday evenings and Saturday mornings and even on holidays, the young boys had the honor of assisting him, taking over parts of the service.

Cantor Oppenheim was a typical German schoolmaster. He paid great attention to detail: every phrase had to be exactly right. He wouldn't accept half-hearted attempts. His standards were very high. I never forgot what he taught me. I will always be grateful to him.

I continued bravely on at the Gymnasium in Wattenscheid, while my brothers were pupils at a Jewish school in Gelsenkirchen. They went there by streetcar every day. Benno was becoming a tall, athletic fellow with red hair, fair skin and large brown eyes. People often admired Benno's deep, dark eyes and Eddi's thick, wavy, black hair. When Benno was little, Eddi and I used to tease him because he was the youngest. As he grew older and more wiry, we backed off. He was excellent at sports and gymnastics; he became a better soccer player than Eddi, who was good at every sport. Though I was keen about most athletics, my physical skills didn't match my enthusiasm, so my participation was limited. Besides, when I was twelve, I began to wear glasses due to my near-sightedness. At first I was ashamed of them and used to put them on only in class to see the board, but after a while I had to wear them even to play soccer, risking their falling off. So as time went on, I was usually found in the cheering section at soccer games.

My brothers and I, especially Benno and I, were soccer fanatics. Our favorite team was *Schalke 04*, who won the German championship several times during the 1930's. Another team we followed was *Höntrop SV*, whose stadium was within walking distance of our home. Benno and I spent many a Sunday afternoon at the games, often to the consternation of our parents. I knew the players' scores better than Benno did, but Benno knew them better than Eddi did. Eddi liked to do things rather than talk about them, whereas Benno compared records, discussed moves and played well himself.

We all did well in school. But I felt increasingly uneasy at the local Gymnasium. The usual salutation between teachers and students had become *Heil Hitler* and Nazi songs were sung fervently at school assemblies. I knew it was only a matter of time before I'd be expelled or something worse would happen. So in 1935 I told my father I wanted to join my brothers at the Jewish school; I couldn't go on at the Gymnasium. My father tried to dissuade me because of the level: the Jewish school was just a primary school with a number of higher grades, not like a Gymnasium. Finally he gave his consent.

Soon I acknowledged to my father that I would prefer a Gymnasium after all. In a few months I quit the Jewish school and enrolled at the Gymnasium in Gelsenkirchen. Other Jewish boys from the area were there, and this lessened the pressure from Nazi sentiments and ideology.

Germany was openly re-arming in 1935 and many armaments were produced in our region. Hitler began to urge the nation to protect itself in case of war by building bomb shelters which the government would subsidize. Accordingly, in 1935 my father applied for a subsidy and installed a shelter in our cellar. It was completely furnished and stocked with dried foods and other necessities. Living under extreme conditions was becoming imaginable, even palpable.

Some time in 1935 a letter arrived from Australia, like a voice from another world. It was from a man named Rosen who had emigrated. He offered to reciprocate my father's generosity: he had toiled in the coal mines near us until my father had given him a start in business. He was now successful in Australia, and was confident that my father would do well there too. He urged my father to let him help us secure immigration papers. The man's gratitude and the offer astonished my father; in fact, when I think about it now, it seems to me it truly alarmed address on the envelopes I would handle wonderingly. My father's response was consistently negative; he claimed he knew very little about Australia. "Where's Australia? What's in Australia?" he would mutter.

Then he ordered us to stop discussing the subject. He refused to move. He never considered his chance properly. I can hardly bear to think how he must have begun to regret it very soon afterwards.

Other people were leaving. In 1936 my bachelor uncle, Mischel, who lived in our house and managed our furniture store, decided to pack up and get out of Germany. He went to live in Israel, where he died in the 1960's. I never saw him again.

Later that year a fire broke out in our clothing store and a section of it burned. My father was arrested and accused of setting the fire—improbable, since sales were booming!

A master tailor working for my parents was living over the store as we were. He and his wife occupied the apartment next to ours. His name was Erwin Schrock. His wife, Hedwig, had been a nursemaid in our home at the age of sixteen, in 1923, before Eddi was born. Besides what I remember of the Schrocks in those darkening days, I know the details of their lives quite well because I was able to meet Hedwig and their two children again in Germany in 1981.

Hedwig and Erwin Schrock had virtually become a part of our family. They lived in the annex of our home because my parents wanted them nearby. Both my parents were deeply attached to the Schrocks and the Schrocks had been devoted to them. Baba Shoshi—and Uncle Mischel—had both been very fond of golden-haired Hedwig whose Slavic face regularly burst into radiant smiles; and my mother, an only child, treated Hedwig like a beloved younger sister. Similarly, my father and Erwin were like brothers.

Erwin Schrock came from Stettin in Pomerania, a part of Germany that is now in Poland. In 1921, when he was 22, he began to work for my father and stayed with him from then on. Schrock was capable, good-looking and elegant. He was also an intelligent, independent-minded man. My father trusted him completely and relied on him increasingly in business matters.

After our store burned and my father was arrested, Erwin Schrock checked around the building. He found matches that had evidently been left by whoever had set the fire. He showed these to the police; then they arrested him, too, and charged him with being involved!

My father was kept in the prison near Wattenscheid for four weeks; Schrock was held for two weeks. He appeared as a witness for my father: he testified unsuccessfully in my father's defence.

A concentration camp at Dachau near Munich had been started in 1933. Munich was Hitler's favorite place: he founded the Nazi Party there, not in Berlin, and was very popular in Munich. It was there that he always made his crucial announcements. And it was fitting that he set up his first concentration camp in the suburb of Dachau.

As German newspapers were severely censored by the authorities, we began buying German-language papers from Bern and Zurich and in them we read articles about Dachau. Jews and non-Jews, Communists, Socialists and others who opposed Hitler's policies were being thrown into Dachau. It wasn't a death camp like the later versions, but people were suffering and dying there because of mistreatment, malnutrition and slave labor. This was well known at the time; my parents talked about it at home.

My father wasn't sent to a concentration camp; he was kept in an ordinary jail and underwent the usual prison treatment. Then he and Schrock were released and the whole matter seemed to be put to rest. None of us talked about it afterwards.

After this episode the day's receipts from the stores were kept by Erwin Schrock. By then my father had begun to realize that we were losing our rights, yet he was determined not to be intimidated into leaving Germany. My parents often discussed this question. My father felt there was no reason for him to have to leave; he would go on his own terms or not at all. Losing his property let alone his life were not in his plans.

By 1935-36 it was becoming clearer to him that all might not turn out well. But we were prosperous and, when people are living affluently in the country of their choice or birth, they don't readily detach themselves from it.

More significantly, my father was forty-two years old in 1936. For a man of that age with numerous attachments and dependents, emigration is a most serious decision. Brecht wrote that being a refugee is like suffering a brain hemorrhage. Exile isn't an option that a responsible person chooses lightly.

From late 1935 on, my parents' plan was to send all the children away; I was to go first. After that they would see what happened. They didn't expect events to follow as quickly as they did; they thought they had some time.

I continued at the Gymnasium in Gelsenkirchen until the spring of 1937, then I left. I couldn't have lasted there much longer. It was almost impossible for a Jewish youngster to attend a German Gymnasium; the pressures were becoming overwhelming. The Hitler Youth had already been indoctrinated for several years. To hate Jews was their supreme *mitzvah,* their first commandment. One of their major tenets held that Jews were the cause of their *Unglück,* their misfortune.

Many young Nazis had a mystical feeling about Germany and about having a mission to fulfill. A main aim of this mission was to wipe out all the Jews in Germany. Jews were classified as rats, sewer rats, vermin. Hitler and his propagandists inveighed against Jews constantly. The evidence of this building mountain of propaganda is still there for all to see in the press and posters of the time; the world had never seen its like, a truly modern weapon in ideological warfare.

Schoolmates were baiting me and sneering, "There's no place for you here. Why don't you go to the Holy Land? Why don't you get out of here? We have no use for you. You're responsible for all our troubles." They would become frenzied. It wasn't possible for me to study among them or to be among them any longer.

The German school system has, or at least had, what was called the *Obersecunda Reife,* which was similar to a junior matriculation or intermediate high school diploma. I completed this level in 1937. In another two years I could have sat for the *Arbitur* or senior matriculation.

Hamburg and Cologne—which was closest to us—each had a Jewish Gymnasium that covered only the intermediate level. In Frankfurt and Berlin Jewish Gymnasia offered the higher grades.

I told my father that I couldn't attend a public Gymnasium any longer, that I couldn't stand it. Eddi had gone to Berlin the year before when he graduated from the Jewish school in Gelsenkirchen. In Berlin he was attending an ORT school, a trade school for Jewish boys run by the Organization for Rehabilitation through Training. Since he was already there, my father said, "Try joining Eddi in Berlin." As a result, I applied and was accepted at the *Adath Israel* Gymnasium in Berlin. I was fifteen years old.

CHAPTER V
DEPARTURES

My father accompanied me to Berlin to settle me in. Eddi moved away from the family he'd been boarding with and together we moved into a kosher hotel on the *Kurfürstendamm*. By then Eddi knew his way around the city so I was quickly oriented. Berlin was rather overwhelming but at the same time the anonymity of the big city was a relief in its way.

I began studying at the *Adath Israel* Gymnasium in April, 1937. I found the standards very high: it took me weeks of strenuous effort before I caught up to other students—they were better trained than I was in the basics. At the school in Gelsenkirchen I was easily the best student; the school in Berlin, however, admitted only top students from all over Germany. Many of the teachers, moreover, had taught in German universities but had recently been forced out; they were far more scholarly than the high-school teachers in Gelsenkirchen.

The school comprised a few hundred boys, with thirty-five or forty to a classroom. I was in the *Unterprima*, the next-to-final class. It was a stimulating environment, an exacting one.

Some boys in my class were preparing to write the Cambridge English exam; it could be written in Germany even then. If they achieved high scores, they had a chance to gain admission to Cambridge or Oxford. I knew several from the Gymnasium who accomplished this. In due course my father suggested to me, "Why don't you take the exam? Maybe you could study in England." My parents were always proud of my scholastic ability and had lofty aspirations for me. Hence I began, with direction from my teachers, to drill myself to write the Cambridge exam.

For social life in Berlin, Eddi and I joined a Zionist group, a youth branch of the Mizrachi Organization called *Brith Hanoar*, to which we already belonged at home. An active unit flourished in Gelsenkirchen: I had been the secretary and had met touring national leaders there. Since they were mainly from Berlin, Eddi and I resumed acquaintance with them now.

Some of these youthful Zionists became prominent in Israel later on. Many founded kibbutzim and some served in the government. I remember Josef Burg of Leipzig, who became a long-time cabinet minister in Israel and was a vigorous Zionist organizer when I was in Berlin.

Another person I remember, who attended Adath Israel Gymnasium concurrently with me, was Walter Würzburger; he hailed from Munich. He went on to become one of the most distinguished Orthodox rabbis in North America.

Among students at the Gymnasium the major motivation was to pass exams. I'd been more concerned with the state of Germany while in Gelsenkirchen and Wattenscheid than I was in Berlin. The population was diverse and cosmopolitan and there were many Jews.

Eddi and I felt safer than in a small town where we could be pointed out as almost the only Jews. In Berlin I concentrated on always passing the next exam; I paid little attention to politics.

It was an insular life. My parents weren't there constantly talking about politics with friends and people who dropped by; since my brother and I were living among transient strangers, we spoke about politics with no-one. We scarcely read newspapers or listened to the radio because there seemed to be no point as both were under government control and censorship. Ironically, we became less involved in political events even though we were closer to so many of them.

While we were in Berlin in 1938, our uncle Beryl, his wife and youngest son, whose home was in Oberhausen not far from Bochum, were deported to Poland. From there, by a circuitous route they made their way to Israel, where the two oldest sons had gone a few years earlier. Now our immediate family was the only one left in Germany: all our close relatives had gone. My father's mother was still in Poland and his sister, Gusta, was in Holland with her family. Everyone else had left Europe.

On November 7th, 1938, a junior official in the German embassy in Paris whose name was Ernst vom Rath was shot. His assailant was a teenage Jewish boy. In retaliation for this killing the Nazis proceeded to destroy Jewish property and levy taxes on German Jews.

Kristallnacht, or the Night of the Broken Glass, came on the ninth of November. That night squads of Nazis invaded Jewish neighborhoods. They smashed the building glass. They looted and set fire to Jewish homes, factories, stores, and synagogues.

These depredations struck small towns first, not Berlin. In small towns all the Jewish real estate was pinpointed and blighted; not in big cities.

Berlin was a huge metropolis. There the Nazis focused on limited targets. Eddi and I lived on the Kurfürstendamm, which was and still is one of the main avenues. It was a mixed area, not especially Jewish. Our district was undisturbed so my brother and I were unaware of what was happening around Germany.

We got up to go to school on the morning of November 10th, 1938, as we did any other day. Suddenly the telephone rang with a call from our mother. The time was seven o'clock.

She blurted out that my father had just been arrested again. Alone she didn't know what to do. I don't even remember if she mentioned what had happened to the store, I was so shocked at the news of my father. She told us to come home immediately.

Actually Eddi and I were much safer in Berlin than anywhere else: fewer arrests and less damage occurred there than in any other city in Germany. But my mother had no way of knowing this.

After her call, we hurried home by express train. We arrived in Wattenscheid, reached our gutted store, greeted our haggard mother, and sat down to drink tea in the kitchen. The police turned up soon after and arrested Eddi and me right there.

We were flung into the jail in Wattenscheid. That night we were transferred to Herne, a few kilometres away. Our aunt Rosa, my father's sister, had lived in Herne with her husband and children until they left Germany in the early 1930's.

We were detained in the jail in Herne along with other Jewish boys. One was Walter Nussbaum whose home, like ours, was in another town nearby. We got to know him quickly in those unusual circumstances; many years later my brother would find him again in Israel. And he still maintained his sense of humor: once he said to my grandson, who was on a visit to Israel, "You know where I met your grandfather? In jail!"

Locked up in Herne, I kept wondering where my father was. Then a talkative policeman revealed that we were supposed to be shipped to Sachsenhausen but the camp was full; it couldn't hold any more. He said, "You're lucky, you guys. You're sitting here in Herne, not in Sachsenhausen like the others, the ones ahead of you." My father had been seized ahead of us so I surmised he was in that concentration camp, located near Berlin.

The plan had been to send us, too, to Sachsenhausen but too many people had been crammed there. The Nazis were still somewhat deterred by the effects of overcrowding; later on this didn't enter into their considerations.

After two weeks my brother was released because he was only fifteen. I was held longer, for four weeks, because I was already sixteen; I was regarded as grown up and I suppose they were hoping to find room for me in the grownups' camp.

My mother had been unrelenting in getting me freed. She managed to obtain an exit visa for me to leave the country on a children's transport. Several countries such as Holland, England and Denmark agreed to accept a fixed number of children. I was scheduled for one of those transports. Unluckily I was slated for Holland instead of England, which would have been safer.

Before I left, my father came back; the last day I was in Wattenscheid he returned home. As the guard had said, he had been in Sachsenhausen, one of the worst concentration camps in that period. He looked weak; he had been ill and hadn't yet recovered.

He called me aside on the day I was to leave and said to me, "You're leaving today and I may never see you again. I want to tell you something," pausing, "I'm not supposed to tell you this," he confided. "I had to swear I wouldn't mention it to anyone. If it's discovered that I have, I may be arrested again. But I'll tell you anyway."

He went on. "When I got to Sachsenhausen, the first thing I had to do was stand in line with other men for twenty-four hours. We weren't allowed to go to the toilet. If any of us became unsteady or fell, no-one helped him. Anyone who fainted was shot on the spot and carted away."

My father had been in the army; he had endured severe conditions in the World War. He continued, "There weren't many of us who stood still for that long. Those who did were assigned to barracks and put to work. We had to move heavy rocks all day: we loaded them onto wheelbarrows, pushed them from one place to another and dumped them out. Then we had to reload the wheelbarrows and move the rocks back again! Meaningless work! All day long, every day. And the guards hit us, beat us, and gave us very little to eat. It was inhuman. Many people died."

My father was a strong, robust man but he fell sick in Sachsenhausen and was put in the camp hospital. After four weeks in the camp, he and others arrested on Kristallnacht were released.

Maybe the Nazis freed some individuals to warn Jews to leave Germany: maybe they were trying to drive us away so there would be no need to deal with us further. Next time it wouldn't be so easy; they wouldn't free us again.

My father opened my eyes to Sachsenhausen. Then, "Remember," he drummed into my ears, "whatever you do, never enter a concentration camp. Never put your foot in a concentration camp."

He gave me an extraordinary message. It was one of the most important instructions I ever received—or the most important, because without it there would have been nothing else afterwards. He directed me to do everything I could to stay out of concentration camp. "Because once you're there," he warned, "you'll never get out. It's torture."

He made clear to me what the Nazis were doing in the camps. They debased and weakened people; abuse, starvation and excessive labor were some of the means the Nazis were using in their aim to exterminate Jews.

With that message, my father told me all I needed to know about the concentration camp. Until then I hadn't realized what such a place was like. We had heard about Dachau: we knew that some Jews and Gypsies and nonconformists were imprisoned there. But arrests had been on a relatively small scale. Suddenly we were all candidates for the camps. This was a different matter altogether; it took on another meaning.

My father galvanized me with his warning in December, 1938. It was the last time I saw my father and the last day I saw my mother and my youngest brother, Benno. I never forgot my father's message; I never allowed myself to be deluded. His words were always uppermost in my mind, as long as the horror went on.

My father was too spent to see me off. My mother and brothers escorted me to the station in Gelsenkirchen. There I boarded the train that took me across the frontier into Holland.

CHAPTER VI
ALONE IN HOLLAND

All I had was a small suitcase, the limit we were allowed, along with the ten marks in currency that could be taken out of Germany. My mother had supplemented this with a piece of jewelery—a fine gold chain set with a jewel—which I hid deep in my jacket. That was all I took: some clothing, ten marks and a bracelet.

The train was an ordinary one that ran between Gelsenkirchen and the Dutch border. The flock of Jewish children occupied several railway cars. Gestapo officers climbed aboard to check our papers and, though each of us had a special visa, they were rough and insulting to us.

That transport with children went only as far as Holland. Other trains carried children to England and elsewhere. It was just by chance that some children went here, others there; little forethought determined the destinations. Faced with the choice of letting me rot in jail or bailing me out with a guarantee that I would leave Germany, my mother had snatched at the first refuge offered and that was Holland.

In the evening I crossed into Holland at Winterswijk. But at the border I was interned immediately as an alien! I had been a prisoner in Germany and no sooner did I touch Holland than I was imprisoned again. Of course it wasn't as bad, but it wasn't the warm welcome we might have needed, either.

The institutions involved with refugee children were the Dutch government, local churches and Jewish organizations. The first thing the Dutch authorities did was load us on a bus. We were driven to a town called De Steeg near Arnhem, not far from the German border. There we were taken to a building that housed children in the summer; it was empty for the winter. The location was pastoral and pleasant, overlooking the Ijssel River, a tributary of the Rhine. But the beds in the dormitory were small; they were designed for young children and we were adolescents. The Dutch had expected a transport of little children. They weren't prepared for us. Whatever quarters they had, they made use of. They were undecided about what to do with us and put us in makeshift accommodations.

I was in De Steeg for a couple of weeks, then was shifted to naval quarantine barracks in Rotterdam. There I was interned like a criminal. .

I was feeling lonely and unwanted, so I wrote to my Aunt Gusta, my father's sister who lived in Maastricht, and she came by train to visit me. When finally she reached Rotterdam and the spot where I was, she had exhausted the entire day. She brought a large basket of fruit and chocolates and talked with me for a while. She described the red tape she'd encountered at the gate of the naval installation before she was allowed to see me. But I was so glad she'd persisted—that little bit of family warmth meant a lot.

From Rotterdam I was shifted again, to a youth hostel near Deventer. It was still winter then. The hostel was a recently constructed building occupied only in summer. Its facilities were just right for us but we couldn't stay there long. With summer approaching, youth hostelers were expected and we had to move again.

We were given no schooling; we passed the time doing nothing. I had lost the opportunity to write the Cambridge exam but I tried to continue learning something. I studied Italian and a few other things on my own—anything I could. Classes were started but they weren't well organized: we lacked essential texts and were never in one place long enough to make any headway. During this interval I also began to wear my eyeglasses permanently, maybe because of the stress I was under that I hardly let myself feel.

Occasionally we had visits from Jews in Deventer. One was a man who, from time to time, traveled on business to Maastricht. He offered to take me with him so I could visit my aunt. I asked permission and managed to go with him twice.

The route we followed paralleled the Dutch-German border. Dutch police stopped us several times to check our papers; they appeared to be on high alert.

In Maastricht the man left me with my relatives for a few hours while he attended to business. He picked me up and we returned to Deventer the same night. These excursions were a blessed change from the monotony of internment.

In Deventer I did a little gardening in the spring. I tried to learn to garden; I was bursting to learn something or do something. There was a trade school in the town and after repeated attempts, I succeeded in getting my name on the list to learn plumbing; it seemed to me a useful skill to have. But before I could start apprenticing, I was moved again.

We were taken to an abandoned orphanage in Gouda, the city famous for its cheese. The orphanage was an antiquated building in the centre of the city; dilapidated and dirty, it was a thoroughly unsanitary place. In the dormitories the beds were set close together and outdoors we internees were packed into a small courtyard. Once again we had nothing to fill our time.

Diphtheria flared among us. Some became very sick; all of us were infected. I never developed the disease but I became a carrier. We were tested for diphtheria regularly and if we responded positively we were confined to hospital. In time, I was placed in quarantine in the hospital in Gouda.

I wanted to conceal this worry from my parents; in my letters to them I pretended nothing had happened. In that period, however, each letter from a contagious-disease ward was fumigated and the edges of the envelopes were cut off. I wondered at times if my parents realized what was wrong.

In 1939 my parents struggled to leave Germany through official channels. By then Jews were forbidden to withdraw money from the country, so my father shipped a room-sized container full of valuable precision tools and hand machinery addressed to relatives in Palestine, thinking he and my mother and brother might follow. The shipment reached Italy and no further; there it went astray. The British aggravated the critical situation by blocking entry into Palestine. But no other country would accept Jews, so of course people thought more and more about Israel.

My Aunt Gusta tried to pluck my family out of Germany in 1939 by sending a car with a Dutch driver to pick them up. But my father insisted on having authorization to leave. Stubbornly he cited his German citizenship and military service; he refused to steal away from Germany.

Maybe, after the experience in the concentration camp, he became unrealistic. Maybe his mind could no longer take in what was happening. Or maybe he simply gave up; he lost his gusto. I phoned them from Holland sometimes and they could phone me; the distances were short. I still had some hope, though it was slowly diminishing. There was no longer any way they could legally leave Germany.

My youngest brother could have left with Eddi on the children's transport. In May 1939 Eddie went to England and Benno could have gone with him, but my mother wouldn't let Benno go. "I'll be alone," she wrote. "There'll be no-one at home. I can't let the three of you go." She seemed so bereft that Benno told her he didn't want to go. My poor mother. She would have to watch her son go through the roundups, the ghetto, the trains, and Auschwitz.

In September 1939 the war broke out. I was still in quarantine in the hospital in Gouda. There a nurse who showed some compassion for us said to me one morning, "War broke out today." Then she brought me a newspaper.

Shortly after that I received a letter from my parents. They told me they had moved from Wattenscheid to Dortmund. The move disturbed me and filled me with dread. I told the nurse, "This is the last time I'll ever hear from them. This is the end of it." She tried, nonetheless, to console me. "Don't say that. You never know," she said. But I was very close to correct.

Much later on I learned that, after Eddi and I had left home, Nazis loitered outside our stores. They badgered the Schrocks with remarks like, "Did the Jews rake in money today?" They threatened to blow up the stores. They harassed Hedwig and called her "Jew-wife" because of her friendship with Jews.

Then one day trucks drew up and removed all the goods from our stores. My parents and Benno were ordered to live in a small room behind the Schrocks' apartment. They were forbidden to work from then on. Someone was appointed by the Nazis to administer our property. So much of the whole Nazi fabrication came down to property at bottom—it always did.

When war broke out the Jews in Wattenscheid were forced to move into the *Gemeindehaus*. From there they were taken to a ghetto in Dortmund. My parents and Benno had two rooms, a bedroom and sitting room, in a house with many other Jews.

Later that year, because I was only a carrier of diphtheria and wasn't sick, the Dutch officials decided it was too expensive to keep me in hospital. I was transferred to the harbor area of Amsterdam to a quarantine station normally used by seamen. The barracks and huts were very old. I stayed there in isolation for three months with nothing whatever to do.

Having been a member of the Brith Hanoar, which is part of the Bachad (Brith Chalutzim Datiim), a Mizrachi or religious Zionist organization, I established contact with the group in Amsterdam. Members of the organization came to all the detention centres looking for volunteers to prepare to go to Palestine. The group operated two kibbutzim in Holland, one near Amsterdam and one in the northern province of Friesland. I volunteered to join one of these, to go on *hachshara* or preparation to train myself for collective farm life. The *hachshara* in the north was in Franeker, a town near Leeuwarden, the capital city of Friesland. That one accepted me.

But first I had to be cleared of diphtheria germs. There were no antibiotics or penicillin at that time; my own body had to destroy the infection. I was kept with other infected people so, even if I overcame the disease, I could be reinfected. But once my system had successfully resisted the germs, my body developed some immunity.

December 1939 was exactly a year after I had left Germany. I had spent a whole year in Holland doing absolutely nothing—not educating myself, just wasting time. Besides that, I contracted a contagion due to poor conditions—overcrowding, inadequate food and substandard housing.

Before my release I had to to sign a plethora of documents. Finally I was granted temporary residence and a work permit. I gained release from custody in December 1939. All of a sudden I was a free person. I still had a German passport with a swastika on the cover and a large J for Jude, Jew, stamped inside. But I had Dutch resident status. I was accepted; I was legal. I could walk in the open air. I could breathe. I had nothing but my papers, yet I felt wonderful.

CHAPTER VII
ON *HACHSHARA* IN FRIESLAND

And so I joined the *hachshara* in the small town of Franeker, about twenty kilometers west of Leeuwarden and a short way from Harlingen. This was an isolated region of Holland, with its own marked dialect and its own distinctive character. The land is very flat and close to the sea, a windy, lonely landscape.

Friesland is rich farming country with excellent farmers. They were very hard-working, grim and taciturn; they barely spoke under any circumstances. One of the few remarks they made to me regularly was a proverb on the weather. It went:

Morgen root
Brengt water in der sloot.

It means, a red morning brings water in the ditch. That is, if the sky is red in the morning, it's going to rain.

Conditions were difficult for the Fries farmers. They rose at four in the morning and worked steadily until six in the evening, laboring almost without pause. It was quite a 'preparation' for a town-type like myself.

We were a group of about twenty-five young people, fifteen boys and ten girls. Most of the girls worked in the house; a few were apprentice gardeners with a horticulturist. The boys worked on farms. Our organization leaders demanded that we train hard, grow tough and learn to be skilled farmers from the Friesians.

We all lived together in one building. Our house was the former train station of Franeker; the tracks had been removed and the place had been vacant until we came. Our organization adapted it for our use: the ticket office became the kitchen and the waiting room a boys' dormitory, while the girls slept in a room upstairs. We each had our essential bicycle which we stored in a shed beside the house.

At 3:30 in the mornings we sallied forth on our bicycles; we were obliged to be on the farms at four o'clock when the farmers began milking. It snows in Friesland in winter and I often couldn't see where the road was and I landed in an icy ditch almost every day.

There was a main road with bicycle paths, as there are all over Holland to this day, where I could pedal quite safely. But I had to turn off and struggle for five to ten kilometers along narrow, rutted back roads flanked by wide ditches. In that part of Europe farm buildings are placed far out in the fields; they're not clustered together. Back roads, in particular, weren't cleared of snow early in the morning; I couldn't really tell where a road was and where a ditch was.

Country life was completely new to me; the closest I had ever come was my idyllic childhood summer in Galizia, in Poland. But now I had just emerged from quarantine. I had done nothing for a whole year; in any event I had never worked physically hard in my life. In Germany I had just been a student, chiefly of language and classics. I had grown up in what was then the most technically advanced region of Europe and possibly of the world. Afterwards I had lived in Berlin, still one of the most cosmopolitan of cities despite the Nazis. And suddenly I was thrown into a grind of hard physical labor with people who seldom talked to me. Even when they spoke, I couldn't understand what they were saying: they talked Friesian whereas I only knew some Dutch. In the year I was interned I had learned a little: it was the one single thing I could learn. But these people were Fries and spoke their own dialect, or language, perhaps—it was so different from standard Dutch. They always called me *Jod,* or Jew; they never called me by my name. They had no respect for me. They were very narrow people who weren't at all accustomed to strangers.

They disliked the Dutch. And we were Jews, urban Jews. They didn't know what to make of us: they seemed to think we were demons or some other weird creatures. We worked for them for a pittance; they compromised on that. They had dirt cheap labor and we had our 'training.' They never made us feel at home. They seemed generally ill-tempered and nasty .

It was difficult to gain the Friesians' confidence but once we did, they became somewhat more friendly toward us. They were not really willing to teach us, though this varied with each farmer: some were more patient than others. The one I worked with first was a youngish man. I wasn't the strongest fellow around and he continually discouraged me. "You'll never learn how to milk," he droned. "You'll never become a farmer. You'll never learn it; you're wasting your time." He made me feel most unhappy. I asked myself, "What am I doing here? I'll never be a farmer! I'm working my heart out for nothing."

I hated going out at 3:30 in the morning only to tumble into a ditch every time. The whole endeavor was ridiculous. I was sorry I had undertaken the training. But I had no alternative: if I had quit, I would have been interned again. I was only set free to work on the hachshara.

We were expected to spend about a year on one farm before being allowed to rotate; we had to establish our tenacity. Many Jews at that time believed that persistence alone proved a person's value. An ideological glorification of labor had affected us, too: Zionist groups exalted manual labor, reversing the centuries-old trend of Jews as merchants and scholars.

I was lucky to have a few warm-hearted friends. One of them was a rabbi, Yehoshua Wolf. He had been a rabbi in Berlin; I remembered hearing of him there.

I was eighteen years old, the youngest on the kibbutz. Rabbi Wolf must have been about thirty. He gave *shiurim*, or lessons, and I was a very good student; he liked me because I was the most intellectual in the group.

Yehoshua Wolf was a man who had two left hands. He couldn't do any manual work passably so he spent his time studying. As a result he was ridiculed by some of our members, but I respected him. To me he was a learned man with a great reservoir of knowledge.

Another close friend on the kibbutz was Aaron Rath. He too was from Berlin. He'd attended the university there but he was also skilled at manual work. He told me often to just keep at it, stick to it, and I'd be a farmer as well as a scholar. Every day Rath said, "I'm going to measure your shoulders now." Then he'd take out his measuring tape and stretch it across my back.

"You see?" he'd exult. "Your shoulders are already broader than they were yesterday! You get stronger when you work." And actually, what he said was true. "Every day you get stronger. I know it from myself" And he'd display his muscles. He always made me feel better. "Work! Work! Don't take any notice of what the farmer says." He'd clown and play little tricks to encourage me and cheer me up.

A shortage of nutritious food was a serious problem on the kibbutz. We ate only kosher meat and received provisions from Amsterdam every week. However, we never had enough to satisfy the appetites of young people employed in heavy labor. I was hungry much of the time. But no doubt about it, I was getting tougher. Things were actually starting to look up a bit.

The *hachshara* included both refugees and Dutch citizens: half the members were Dutch so it wasn't like a refugee camp. It wasn't set up for refugees; it had existed for several years before we joined it. A number of individuals had already gone to Palestine from the *hachshara* and when I became part of it, some members had already been training for one or more years. The Dutch Jews were far more at ease than the rest of us. They understood the language and could pick up the dialect quite well. They felt at home. They often helped us out, speaking to the farmers on our behalf.

I encountered my distant cousin Moishe Heller in Franeker. Like Rabbi Wolf, he was ten or twelve years my senior. The Hellers had lived in Hannover in Germany; I knew of them from my parents, but I had never met any of them. When I discovered that Moishe Heller was related to my mother, he took some interest in me. He too encouraged me and helped me to persevere. "You know, it's tough for all of us," he said. He had been in Franeker for some time and was considerably fitter than I was. He had already switched to his second farmer, one more likable than mine.

They were mainly dairy farmers in Friesland. On the first farm where I worked, my principal job was milking cows. It may look easy but it's not, believe me. You have to learn the technique and you have to develop the right muscles. But I finally got it despite my complaints.

The prospect of reaching the farm each day was discouraging nevertheless; it was so far from where we lived. Pedaling there in winter continued to be a battle against wind and snow. I started milking the cows at four in the morning. Then I fed the animals and cleaned the stable. Next I prepared more fodder and attended to other chores. In the early afternoon I repeated the same routine of milking, feeding and cleaning. In warmer weather, in between the stable chores I worked in the fields haying or spreading manure. I was busy until six in the evening. I had one or two hours of rest during the day.

I never entered the farmer's house; I was relegated to the stable. A typical Friesian farmhouse was very large: the small front part, which had a tiled roof, was the farmer's home. The large back part had a thatched roof and contained a barn and a high hayloft. I never saw the kitchen or the inside of the house. I was strictly a farmhand. Even the other farmhands were contemptuous of me at first because they couldn't figure out who or what I was. But after a while I got friendly with some of them. The farmers, however, never invited me into their homes. I never got anything from them, not even a kind word. Each day I brought my own bread and my own thermos bottle. I was paid about two dollars a week. It was a rough life—but at least a peaceful one.

CHAPTER VIII
THE INVASION OF HOLLAND

Every Friday afternoon our group stopped work early to go to the municipal bath. There we bathed, showered and donned our best clothes. Then we hurried to our house where we held our Friday evening service. We sang *zemirot,* or songs, and I learned many new melodies: some sounded strange to me because they derived from Sephardic Dutch Jews but they were very beautiful.

Our *Shabbat*, or Sabbath, services on Friday evenings and Saturdays were very pleasant and informal. Often we were joined by a Jewish psychiatrist from the psychiatric hospital in Franeker. When he was obligated to say *kaddish*, the mourner's prayer for the dead, we congregated at his home on the Voorstraat in the centre of Franeker. Usually, though, we set up a chapel in the dining room of our house. The rabbi officiated and delivered a sermon: he gave lessons on the *sidra,* the Torah reading of the week.

On Sundays we resumed our labors at four in the morning; we milked the cows early and again in the afternoon but we were free in between. The people of Franeker and surroundings went to church and so we did a half day's work on Sundays.

This routine continued smoothly throughout the winter of 1939-1940 and into the spring. Slowly I grew stronger. I coped with the work more easily as time went on.

We listened to the radio and heard rumors daily that Germany was planning to invade. No-one believed it. Holland had been neutral for a long time: the Dutch had stayed out of the 1914-1918 conflict and they hadn't engaged in a war in Europe for several hundred years. There was no viable indication that the Germans would invade Holland.

Then suddenly it happened, on May 10, 1940. I was at work on a farm when I heard the report. The farmer repeated an announcement he'd heard on the radio: the Germans were crossing the border. Troops were invading Holland from different directions.

Without hesitation I told the farmer, "I have to go back and talk to my colleagues." I felt we had to do something. I and some of the others had fled the Nazis and here they were, coming after us again. Past outrages would recur.

I almost flew on my bicycle to the *hachshara*, arriving around ten o'clock in the morning. A few others had come back. One was my cousin Moishe Heller, a person I looked up to for advice and support.

I talked to him and said to him and then to others, "Look, we have to get out of here fast, take our bikes and try to reach the other side of Holland. Maybe we can board a boat to England. We have to clear out, otherwise we'll be trapped; we may never get away."

Moishe was opposed to the idea. He was a cautious man who tried to plan every move carefully. "Let's use our heads. Let's reason things out," he said. He thought I was panicky.

I said to him, "Don't pretend the Nazis use reason. They're not reasonable people." I knew their mentality. I had gone to school with the Hitler Youth. Their devotion to the Führer had reached such proportions that I believed they would go to extremes for him. And my father's warning echoed in my mind.

Most of the others in our group, especially the Dutch, were cool to my proposal. They didn't know what the Nazis were like.

A fellow from Bavaria was part of our group. Even through the thickness of Dutch, one could detect his Bavarian accent. Benno Jacobs was his name.

Benno and I decided to mount our bikes and pedal as far as we could go in the direction of Amsterdam or Rotterdam. We would try to ship out from one of the harbors on the coast or from the Rotterdam area. We wanted to escape from the German onrush.

We were the only ones who left. We snatched our bikes and rode away. We took nothing with us—no food or change of clothing. It didn't occur to us.

At about eleven o'clock that morning we hurried away, pedaling furiously. We intended to move out of Friesland, the northeast end of the country, and get down to the western side. Holland was gripped by confusion and we had no information about what was happening.

From Harlingen we pedaled on down the coast. About twenty kilometers from where we'd started, we came to a very long causeway: it crossed the Zuider Zee, a body of water which is now called Ijsselmeer. We saw troops beside the causeway but paid no attention to them; we barreled ahead.

We were stopped at the causeway. The soldiers asked who we were; they demanded to see our identification papers. We had no papers; we had left them in Franeker.

The soldiers were stopping everyone. They were attempting to cull German invaders, including those who had parachuted in wearing cassocks and dresses with machine guns under their clothes. We found out later that paratroopers, masquerading in that fashion, had occupied Rotterdam

We were arrested by the soldiers at the causeway. Our bicycles were confiscated. We were seated in a corner near the water and several soldiers stood guard over us.

For a few hours we sat there wondering what would be done with us. We tried to explain who we were, that we weren't German soldiers or spies; we were German refugees, Jewish refugees. We protested to our guards that we would never help the Germans conquer Holland. But the Dutch soldiers were edgy and excited; they ignored what we said. They didn't believe us. They kept on insisting that we were German spies. There was mass shock and bewilderment that day so we could hardly blame them for not believing us. All of Holland was in turmoil. The Dutch hadn't fought a war in so long that they were completely unprepared. The German attack had taken them by surprise.

After a few hours, a bus appeared and we were ordered onto it. It was driven around in a zigzag course to numerous villages, picking people up. At first Benno and I were the only civilians on the bus, then other people were collared. We didn't know who was being picked up or why; we tried to guess who they were, but we couldn't be sure.

Suddenly we heard German planes overhead: they started bombarding the road we were driving on. Machine-gun fire almost hit the bus. With Dutch soldiers guarding it and some of them standing upright in the doorway, clinging to the frame, it had surely looked like a military vehicle. A security vehicle was tailing us, too.

The planes flew on and gradually the bus filled up. We crossed the long causeway from Friesland into northwest Holland. Once again we were strafed on all sides.

We drove on. Finally we came to a city called Hoorn, north of Amsterdam—an old prison fortress surrounded by water. We stopped.

We were hustled off the bus and into a cellar deep inside the fortress where we were locked in small, dark cells. We remained there for three nights and two days. We got no food; we saw nobody.

Benno and I were sharing a cell with several other men, but we never spoke to them. It was dark, we couldn't see anyone clearly and we knew that we had to be very careful. We were wary of everyone so we scarcely talked and we barely slept.

There were loud explosions nearby. We heard artillery fire and bombardments. At least we were safe from bombs deep in the fortress; it wasn't likely we'd be hit down there.

In the morning of the third day, we were all led upstairs. And who was there? German army officers! They shook hands with each one of us and congratulated us on having survived the bombing. Then they subjected us to speeches about the war and the German empire that now had been enlarged. Holland had now become part of the German empire, they said, and they were looking forward to our collaborating with them in assimilating Holland and incorporating it into the thousand-year empire.

They spoke on and on. Meantime we were served hot coffee and food! We were ravaged with hunger...

Ultimately we found out for certain who our companions were: they were all Dutch Nazis and German infiltrators. We had been thrown in with them! The paradox of paradoxes was that, on the fifteenth of May, we were free men in Holland and freed by the German army! The officers even offered us a lift to Amsterdam in a German army truck. We climbed on the truck and a German army driver took us to Amsterdam. Two German Jews liberated in Holland by the German army—it was rich, though we still didn't feel like laughing. Our identity was never even questioned by the Germans. They were on top of the world and all was going according to their plan.

We arrived in Amsterdam to find it completely deserted. It was like a ghost town; there was no-one in sight. The inhabitants had gone into hiding or run away to the country. Benno and I roamed the streets looking for a human being but we couldn't find anyone.

We went to the head office of our organization. At length some people showed up there. They were mystified by our presence. When we told them what had happened, they gaped and shrugged their shoulders as though we had concocted the story. They just couldn't believe it.

We decided to return to Franeker, since there seemed to be nothing else to do. But all transportation had stopped, so we stayed in Amsterdam for six days until trains were moving again.

At that time the Germans were engrossed in maneuvers in Belgium and France; they weren't much interested, it seemed, in the civic setup in Holland. Benno and I managed to get back to Franeker without incident and found all our colleagues still there. Nothing had happened to them.

CHAPTER IX
OCCUPATION 1940-41

I resumed my work on the farm as if nothing had happened. The summer was lovely that year. There was scarcely a sign of military occupation. We seldom saw a German in our corner of Friesland. Once in a while a patrol passed along the highway: our house was on the Harlingerweg, the road to Harlingen; motorcycles with sidecars would clatter down the road infrequently but the Germans neither stopped nor talked to us. Not much happened. The summer was a quiet one.

I changed to another farm at the end of the season. Moishe Heller had worked there and recommended the place to me: it was easier work than I had been doing and more diversified. Distance was the only drawback: the farm was much farther away from where we lived than my first one. I spent more than an hour traveling there. It was north of Harlingen at Sexbierum close to the sea. Fall and winter wore on and often I had to cycle straight into stiff sea winds.

Still, I liked working there because I learned more than just how to milk. Plowing and field work with horses and growing potatoes were part of the job. The farmer was a specialist in potatoes. The production of seed potatoes was a major industry in Friesland. Friesians grew some of the best potatoes anywhere, many for export. There wasn't much trade then because of the war but normally their potatoes went all over the world.

I was very impressed with the way the potato industry was organized. Every few weeks an inspector would come into the field. He scrutinized every plot and assigned grades A, B or C: if the plants were tall and dark green with no sign of disease, the potatoes were given a high grade. The higher the grade, the better the price, of course. So farmers worked for high grades and good returns.

The Dutch also established courses in milking and milkers had to pass examinations. The farmers paid workers according to their grades. All in all, the farming industry in Holland was extremely well operated.

Besides working and learning how to farm, I took all the courses in religion offered by Rabbi Wolf in the evenings. We studied *Mishnah*, the oral common law, and *Gemara*, debates on the common law, and also Jewish history. Every *Shabbat* we discussed the Biblical portion of the week. Rabbi Wolf was a gifted teacher and, because of his association with us, I had a rare opportunity to learn.

There was a furniture factory next to the station house where we lived. Many carpenters worked there. What I really wanted was to acquire a trade or profession other than farming so I talked to some of the factory staff; they were ready to take me on as an apprentice. I proposed this to our group, arguing that in Israel carpenters would be needed as well as farmers; all kinds of skills are required to build a country. Our leaders brought my request to the highest council in Amsterdam. The council discussed and opposed it: the reason they gave was that the organization wanted all of us to know how to farm. So I had to keep on working as a farm laborer. I was well into my gruelling second year.

At the same time our group noticed that I was talented in discussions on religion. It was decided finally that the group might benefit from sending me to rabbinical seminary in Amsterdam to study for a year—not to take a degree but to learn. Then the group would have a second person who could direct religious studies. Rabbi Wolf sponsored me strongly for this. He contended that we needed young people trained to lead discussions, interpret the Torah and teach others.

This time the leaders in Amsterdam agreed. They voted in favor of my coming to Amsterdam for a year to study at the seminary. I was never to go. Something else would intervene.

In September of 1941, for *Rosh Hashana* and *Yom Kippur*, the High Holidays, I visited my Aunt Gusta Schmidt and her family. I spent many holidays with them. To get from Franeker, close to the most northerly point of Holland, to Maastricht, near the most southerly point, I had to cut right across the country, a trip that took a full day by train. There were German soldiers guarding the stations but there was no interference with the daily life of ordinary civilians, as far as I could see. And so I made my way to my aunt's house without incident.

Aunt Gusta was devoted to me because she had lived with my father when she first emigrated from Poland. She had kept house for him when he was struggling to build up his business and she felt very close to him. She tried to do whatever she could to make me feel comfortable in her home. Now and then she also sent me money by mail. She always said my father had sent it for me by courier but by that time I rarely got any notes or letters from home so I don't know if this was true. She may have been giving me money of her own.

She was strikingly good-looking, with black hair, dark brown eyes and clear skin. Her features were small and neat, characteristic of our family. She was slender and graceful with a riveting presence—a person who drew you to her. Besides this, she was unusually kind and generous. She was genuinely good, like my father. He was an open-handed man who would empty his pockets for someone in need without expecting thanks. Tante Gusta was exactly the same. She had tremendous warmth and humanity. Whenever I came to visit her in Maastricht, she treated me like a prince. I never had such treatment from anyone else. She radiated the same benevolence as my father.

There were five cousins, three boys and two girls. One had the unusual name of *Schneewittchen*, which is German for Snow White. The boys were my age and a year or two younger; we always had fun together. The family had been in Holland since 1933 or 1934. When they lived in Germany, they had barely scraped by but in Maastricht they had done quite well. Her husband owned a furniture store and seemed more than adequately successful. He was a devout and humorless man.

Visiting Tante Gusta's home was my holiday from hard labor. The food was traditional and plentiful: baked carp, chicken noodle soup, roast chicken or boiled beef, potato pancakes, red cabbage, and sponge cake. Her meals were much more satisfying than those on the *hachshara*, where we lived on bread, milk and boiled vegetables, mainly potatoes, peas or beans. Doing farm labor and eating little meat is a debilitating combination: it was a struggle to work hard steadily when our diet lacked sufficient protein. Under the German occupation, it was particularly difficult to get kosher meat to the tiny community of Franeker; in Maastricht, on the other hand, kosher meat was still readily available.

That *Rosh Hashana* and *Yom Kippur*, my aunt and uncle were quite concerned about the occupation. I met several other Jews from Maastricht at their home. No visible action had been taken against anyone, but the ominous mood was overwhelming.

Back on the *hachshara* after the holidays, in October or November 1941, our group was called to the Gestapo headquarters in Leeuwarden. All of us had to appear there with our visas and passports. The Gestapo examined our papers and asked a number of questions; then they let us go. Prior to this we had had to report a few times to the small police station in Franeker.

On the *hachshara* we foolishly believed that we would be able to leave Holland, that somehow the Nazis would let us go. In Germany they had permitted emigration until late in 1939. But then the British blocked immigration to Palestine. Also, with a war going on, there was now no longer any way to travel to Palestine—there were no passenger ships, no civilian traffic. It had become almost impossible to get there.

As the war escalated, the chances of fleeing from Holland came close to zero. No other country provided asylum. The Germans closed the borders; they stopped all exodus.

The Nazis began to establish the *Joodse Raad*, the Jewish Council, in Holland. Nobody knew what the purpose was to be-we didn't realize what was going on. But slowly rumors circulated that the Jewish Council was 'recruiting,' At first it was young people between the ages of twenty and thirty who signed on for 'work camps:' the rumor was that they would work for the Germans in war industries. We heard these rumors but way up in Franeker we were never part of that recruitment.

I was not able to phone my parents any more. I think long distance calls were restricted to military business. I wrote letters to them and they wrote to me; sometimes the letters got through. My parents never wrote much: they were under surveillance and letters were censored. But I read between the few lines that they weren't doing well. I worried about how they were living from day to day, how well they were eating, how their health and their spirits were holding up, what treatment they were being subjected to.

All the Jews in the Ruhr Valley had been rounded up and herded into a ghetto in Dortmund. Jewish-owned businesses were closed. My parents were not allowed to work; they couldn't earn any money. They were living in Dortmund on the same street as some distant relatives. My youngest brother, Benno, was there with them. He was supporting them, learning to be a carpenter by working in heavy construction for some entrepreneur—at least, that was what they told me. In 1941 Benno was just sixteen years old.

In the fall of 1941 I received a letter from Eddi through the International Red Cross. Surprisingly, it came from Canada; I was astonished to see that! Until then I had thought Eddi was in England because he had gone there in 1939; that was the last I'd heard from him—a long time not to hear from your brother. He wrote, however, that he had been interned in England because he was a German citizen and had been shipped from England to Canada along with other German Jews and German prisoners of war. Now he was in an internment camp near a place called Fredericton in New Brunswick. He was working in the forest, felling trees. He'd had to use a Red Cross form letter, without much room, for information, but that thin lifeline to my brother was a wonderful event. I could only think how glad I was that he was well—and well away from Europe.

I was still on the *hachshara*. I had recently begun working on a farm very close to where we lived: I was able to go home for breakfast. This was one of the placements that most of our group tolerated better because it was on the Harlingerweg just beyond the psychiatric hospital, about three minutes from the house by bicycle. It was also a clean place to work and the owner was fair-minded. I inherited the job from a colleague because I'd become an excellent milker. The farmer Van der Berg had a large herd of cows so the job required an experienced hand. I was happier with the job mainly because of the proximity: I didn't have to cycle for an hour or worry about falling into ditches in the early morning.

I was working out in the fields one cloudy day in late 1941, in cool, rainy weather such as we often had in Friesland. By then the solid manure that had been collected all year had grown into a bulky pile. Liquid manure also had accumulated in the ground in large containers that were cemented and covered: this liquid had to be sprayed on the land with hoses attached to special carts.That autumn morning we were trucking solid manure out to the fields. A crew was loading the manure onto two or three carts; when the first cart was full, a farmhand drove it to the field, unloaded the manure and came back for the second load. The carts were operating in tandem. I was driving a cart pulled by two horses. Suddenly, when I was out in the field with a load, the horses shied, then went wild. The cart, manure, horses and I flew into a ditch. I could have been killed—the cart or horses could have fallen on me. Miraculously, I landed on top and slowly I sank into freezing water.

When I failed to return for a while, the farmer grew suspicious. He came after me and found me near the ditch—I had scrambled out by that time. The horses were out; the wagon was partly smashed. The farmer tried to retrieve whatever he could; then he told me to go home, change my clothes, get a hot drink and keep warm. He saw that I was shivering and, obviously, feeling a bit sick.

So I went home and changed my clothes. Then I drank hot tea and got into bed to warm up. It was about eleven in the morning. I fell asleep.

At about two o'clock I woke up. I heard boots, German boots, I realized right away, marching onto the former station platform in front of our house. A small army was assembling there. I thought, "This is it. They've come to pick us up." We'd been wondering why they never bothered us.

I pulled the blankets over my head and played dead. I thought, "Maybe they won't see me." The room was large, the main waiting room, with twelve or more beds in it; some were bunk beds.

But of course they spotted me and one of the officers, in typical Nazi fashion, raised his foot and shoved me with his boot. Then he kicked me. Finally he ordered me in German to step up, get up immediately. He was barking orders.

The others stalked the room and tore it apart. They opened cupboards and knocked things out. We had little in them but anything we did have was thrown to the floor. Beds were overturned. They combed through everything.

Then the officer said to me, "You line up with the others." Some of the soldiers went upstairs to the room where we stored a few bags of food and cans of vegetables.

Soon these soldiers came out screeching, "See what these Jews are hoarding? They're hoarding food! Hoarding this!" We had barely enough to eat for the next day; there was absolutely nothing to hoard. We had a few bags of beans and potatoes. "Hoarding and hoarding and hoarding!"

They lined us up on the platform. We stood there for a couple of hours. They were waiting for everyone to return from work. They were rounding us up, obviously to take us away.

The Dutch police were there too. They were helping the Germans by describing the region to them and informing them where all our members worked. They went as far as to fetch some back themselves: in fact, they rounded up quite a few. I was struck then by the close cooperation between the Dutch police in Franeker and the Germans. A lesson to bear in mind.

I was standing in line, still jittery from my tumble into the ditch that morning. German soldiers were posted all around.

In desperation I spoke in German to a soldier and said, "Look, I have almost nothing on. Can I go inside and get my jacket? Can I go and get my jacket?"

He answered, "No. No. What do you need a jacket for? You won't need a jacket where you're going."

I asked him again in spite of what he'd said: he seemed to have a little sympathy, especially when he heard me speak in German. And sure enough, the next time I asked him, he grumbled, "Alright, go ahead. And come back fast." The Nazis were always ordering you to do everything *schnell*, fast. So I did.

I scurried into the station house. The place was a wreck. Instead of looking for my jacket, I raced to the back door: every railway station has two doors. The back door of this station house was blocked by a heavy case; if I could move it aside and open the door, I might get away.

On occasion even weak people can summon unusual strength. My hair was short, unlike Samson's, but I had more of it then than I have today. And like sightless, enfeebled Samson I exerted enough force to move that case.

I didn't wait for anything. I opened the door and looked neither to left nor right. I simply threw myself out.

There was a ditch behind the house. In one jump I was in that ditch.

The guards had noticed nothing. They stood one at each end of the back of the building but facing the front; they expected nothing to happen at the back.

I listened for a moment, waiting for reactions; then I crept along the ditch. Tall grasses and water clogged the way. I knew that in two hundred metres or so I would reach an open field. If I kept my head down and moved quickly and very carefully, I might get away.

I reached the field, then a row of houses nearby. A farm worker acquaintance lived there. I knew the Germans would be looking for me soon: the soldier who had let me go would notice my absence.

An empty kennel stood there with no dog in sight. In a moment I'd decided to hide in it. I crept inside and crouched low. It was roomy, for a kennel!

I stayed there until dark, then decided to move. I thought I might waylay one or two of my friends and try to save them; I hoped they weren't all rounded up.

One fellow always returned late in the evening because he worked on a distant farm. I headed in that direction.

Under cover of darkness I trotted down the road and was lucky enough to intercept him. I told him what had happened.

He was a Dutch Jew, Bram, a big, brawny fellow. He had less difficulty with the local people than I had: on the farm where he worked, for instance, he'd become close friends with a Friesian who owned a little farm of his own. We decided to go to him and try to hide in his barn for a while.

We went to the man and explained why we had come. We persuaded him to go to Franeker that night to find out what was going on. He knew everyone in town.

He did, and dropped in at a local bar and talked to people gathered there. The day's event was the most exciting thing to hit Franeker in years; the town was buzzing because of it. Townsfolk said all the Jews had been rounded up except two: one had escaped and the other couldn't be found. The Germans were looking for both of them. The other Jews were now in prison in Leeuwarden. The old station house was empty; the Germans had ransacked the place.

Bram and I hid out on his friend's farm for two days. We didn't budge. The Germans were hunting for us.

Without question we had to abandon the area. Although the Friesian farmhand backed us a hundred percent and would have concealed us indefinitely, there was no reason for us to stay on. Everything we were linked to was destroyed. Nothing was left.

More importantly, since Dutch police were collaborating with the Gestapo, how much chance did we have? We would have been caught eventually in such a tight little community. Also, by hiding us, the farmhand was running a great risk: at some point someone would have betrayed him.

We decided that on the third day at five or six in the morning we would try to take the first bus out of the neighborhood. From a station further south we would go by train to Amsterdam.

Our plan succeeded. We got away from the farm and left the area on a bus from a village near Franeker. We went first to a town called Sneek. There we saw German guards at the train station but passed them without any questions: our pictures weren't in circulation so nothing conspicuous identified us. Contrary to Nazi belief, they couldn't actually spot a Jew most of the time. We boarded a train to Amsterdam that afternoon.

The first thing we felt obliged to do on arriving in Amsterdam was report to our headquarters. The officials sent us to the Jewish Council, the *Joodse Raad*, which occupied the same building. Our organization respected the purpose of the Council. This was still only 1941.

We presented ourselves at the Council office and the functionary in charge exclaimed, "Oh! You two are here! We've been waiting for you. We've been looking for you."

I said, "What do you mean—'looking for you'?"

"I just had a telephone call," he answered, "from the Chief Rabbi of Leeuwarden. The Gestapo have been in contact with him. They told him that unless you two report voluntarily and give yourselves up, all the others will be shipped to Westerbork." An internment camp established by the Dutch in the late thirties, Westerbork had become a German concentration camp.

I hissed at him, "I'll tell you something. They have twenty-five of us now. If we give ourselves up, they'll have twenty-seven. All that you will achieve is only to send two more Jews to Westerbork instead of two less."

"Shame! Shame!" he cried. "It's your duty to stand with your colleagues, to stand side by side with your comrades! Don't you have any feeling of responsibility?"

I shouted back at him, "My responsibility is to save myself! Bram's responsibility is to save himself! And anyone else that we can. But we can't save the others! I know the Gestapo. It's certainly not my responsibility to cooperate with them! By giving ourselves up we'll achieve nothing, nothing! We would just be helping the Nazis in their filthy work!" I knew this immediately, though I couldn't convince a pompous creature who was either deliberately harmful or a dupe and a fool.

I'm glad to be able to record that our movement supported us completely. Bram and I split up and our officials arranged for me to spend a few days with a Sephardic family by the name of Rodrigues. Distinguished people who were deeply religious members of the renowned Spanish and Portuguese Synagogue of Amsterdam, they were very kind and concerned. But I couldn't stay with them long; they found another place for me.

I moved to the Koster house. Very rich Jews, the Kosters lived in the *Zuid* (south), a wealthy enclave of Amsterdam. Their mansion commanded a sheltered street of imposing single homes off a wide boulevard called Apollolaan,.

Koster was the most eminent professor of accountancy in Holland. Many top students of accountancy in the entire country came to study with him. Furthermore, he directed a busy private firm.

The Kosters had four children; one was mentally disturbed. They had had severe problems with that child and employed a specially-trained nurse solely to care for him.

My arrival on the premises was the direct result of their need for a maid! The house soared several stories high and contained many spacious rooms and bathrooms: they needed somebody to do heavy work—scrub floors, clean carpets, wash windows. By then Jews were no longer allowed to hire any non-Jewish help.

Thus I became a domestic in the Koster house. Semi-cloistered, I couldn't ramble outdoors at will because my rights had disappeared; my name was on the wanted list of the Gestapo.

CHAPTER X
I CHANGE MY NAME TO ELI HART

At that time I devised a stratagem in order to correspond with my parents. Eli Hart was the name of a member of our group in Amsterdam: he was a Dutch Jew who lived beside one of the canals, the Heerengracht in Amsterdam.

I wrote to my parents as usual but my name changed abruptly to Eli Hart and I was living in Amsterdam. I explained nothing to my parents about what had happened; they understood. It must have caused them some worry yet they never asked me why, how, or what. I signed my letters 'Eli Hart' and they addressed me forthwith by that name. And Eli brought me the letters that came to him from my parents. It was November 1941 and Moritz (Moishe) Schnitzer didn't exist anymore.

So began my false identities. I had to adopt such tactics because I was no longer legal: I couldn't use my own name publicly. The Germans weren't looking for me particularly or they could have traced a connection from Schnitzer in Germany to Eli Hart and me in Holland; they had other priorities.

In this period it became mandatory for every Jew to wear a yellow star. I reasoned that, as I was illegal anyway, why wear a yellow star? So I decided not to wear it and never did. This in itself was a dangerous breach of the law but I believed that it was wiser for me to violate it than observe it.

The Kosters were incurring a risk by harbouring me; Koster was a man inclined to take chances. He often travelled to The Hague and Rotterdam on business; he himself never wore the yellow star. He boasted to me: "You don't wear a yellow star; I don't wear it either!" I admonished him for this: "You have more to lose than I have. I have nothing to lose. I'm all alone. No one knows me. People recognize you; you're well-known. You have a family. You're a man of substance. Why do you gamble like this?" He was exposing himself to arrest every moment.

I worked in the Koster house from November 1941, my status slightly higher than that of a maid. It wasn't a pleasant life, but neither was it really unbearable. There was always enough to eat because the Kosters were rich: they bought food on the black market; there was never any shortage.

When I moved to the Koster house, I no longer saw Bram. I didn't know what he was doing. Although his family lived in Amsterdam he dropped out of sight.

Another member of our *haschshara* had been in Amsterdam when the Gestapo rounded us up. He had been on a visit for several weeks, then he had fallen sick; he had stayed in Amsterdam to recover and missed the roundup. But now his name was also on the Gestapo list; he was Menachem (Piefke) Levy.

Piefke was about a year older than I was. Extremely religious, he had belonged to the Agudath Israel movement, an orthodox religious group. He came from Hamburg in Germany and had studied at the Jewish Gymnasium there.

After I moved to the Koster house, I looked for Piefke: I realized he must be living close to me. Indeed he was only three blocks away. He was staying with wealthy and prominent Jews who lived in Amsterdam Zuid. They had done a great deal for him: they had nurtured him back to health and treated him like their own son. He was doing nothing in that house; they simply kept him there.

For months my only recreation was to visit Piefke. In the evening I sneaked over to where he was staying. We talked and played chess: there wasn't much else we could do. I couldn't go about openly: it was dangerous for me even to answer the doorbell because the Gestapo might appear at any time to search the Koster house.

The situation was getting worse and worse. In April 1942 I received a postcard from Dortmund written by my mother and partly by my father. They wrote: "We're leaving for the East. We're leaving to work in the East." The message was obscure. "We're leaving now." It was a brief note in which they said that they and my brother Benno were going to a work camp in the East and I should take care of myself. That was all. It was addressed to Eli Hart.

That was the last mail I ever received from my parents. It was the last time I ever heard from them. April 1942. A card with a few lines that conveyed an awful message.

Piefke's fiancée also disappeared at about this time. Rachel was from Vienna and had been with us on hachshara. She had been caught with the others and sent to Westerbork.

In May 1942 she was allowed to leave Westerbork for a visit to Amsterdam; she was granted a most unusual leave. She stayed with Piefke for a week at the home of the family in Amsterdam Zuid and I saw her there a few times.

Rachel was employed in sewing at the camp in Westerbork; she talked very little about it. One condition of her leave may have been to keep silent about the camp; perhaps she had sworn, as my father had, to tell no one about camp life. But I knew roughly what Westerbork was like; I guessed.

I urged Rachel repeatedly to stay with us. I said to her, "Rachel, don't go back to Westerbork. We'll never see you again if you do." In the strongest way I begged her not to go back. But she always replied, "I have to go back. I promised I would." I told her, "Forget your promise. Don't go back. Stay here. Don't go back or you'll never return." Yet when the week was up she went back. I never saw her again.

At times I went out to try to buy vegetables for the Koster family: shortages had become acute and there wasn't much for sale except radish leaves. People were making use of greens which would normally be thrown away.

There were a number of markets near us. Suddenly the Germans began to sweep through them; Amsterdam became a hunting ground. *Razzia* after *razzia* (raid after raid) took place. The Germans would storm a market and arrest anyone who was wearing the yellow star. I escaped several times simply because I didn't have a star on; everybody who wore one was grabbed, shoved into a police truck, and hauled away.

Piefke and I decided then that we wouldn't survive in Amsterdam Zuid much longer. It was becoming risky for all Jews, even the Dutch-born and resident aliens who had legal visas and permits. The Germans made no distinction: they were seizing everyone.

After the third or fourth raid, at the beginning of July 1942, we moved out of Amsterdam *Zuid.* I moved away from the Koster house and Piefke left his place. We moved in with a family living near the Amstel River in the centre of Amsterdam.

In that district, too, raids were occurring frequently. One day the Gestapo burst into our house; we sprinted to the top of the tall, narrow building and hid ourselves in between the rafters. We escaped detection by sheer luck.

We realized then that we couldn't stay in Amsterdam any longer. The option of emigrating to Israel didn't exist anymore: we couldn't get out of fortress Europe. Switzerland, Spain and Sweden were the only countries one could escape to.

We resolved to make a run for Switzerland; it was the only safe place we thought we could reach. We considered Spain for a while but concluded it was too far away and would probably involve crossing the Pyrenees. Access to Switzerland would be easier. We would travel southward from Holland to Belgium and France, then eastward to the Swiss border.

Piefke had an uncle living on the outskirts of Brussels. We decided to visit him first, gauge the situation around Brussels, and elaborate our plans from there.

Before we left Amsterdam, I wanted to go to Maastricht to say good-bye to the Schmidts. I set out without the yellow star or a permit to travel.

I arrived at my aunt's house; she was overjoyed to see me. Uncle Shalom was hunched in the kitchen praying: he was reading *tehillim* (psalms).

When he saw me, my uncle choked, "What are you doing here?" He knew I was on the run and it was a crime to give me refuge. He asked shrilly, "You came here endangering my family, my children, my wife and me?"

I answered, "Uncle, I'm not staying long. I just came to see my aunt; I especially came to see her. I want to say good-bye; I'm going to try to make my way out of Holland."

Then I thought, "Maybe I can do something for the two oldest boys." I started talking to my aunt; I asked her to allow the two oldest boys to come with me. I talked to them, too, and tried to persuade them to join me.

Their father reacted very strongly. "Who are you to tell the boys to gamble like that, to throw their lives away?"

I countered, "If we don't stand up for ourselves, who will stand up for us? *'Im ain ani li mi li?'* (If I am not for myself, who will be for me?) God helps those who help themselves."

"Oh," he preached back at me, "the will of God will be done one way or another. If God wants us to live, we'll live; if He wants us to die, we'll die. Everything is in the hands of God."

Then he ordered me: "Out of my house this minute; get out of my house. Don't come back with your crazy ideas—talking to people about doing stupid things, especially my sons."

My aunt wept and sobbed. She handed me some money; I left. That was the last time I saw any of the Schmidts.

I returned to Piefke in Amsterdam. Together we collected some road maps and railway charts of Holland, Belgium, and France, mostly the kind used by students and hostellers. Then, still early in July 1942, we bought tickets for Beek in southern Holland, a town close to Maastricht and the Belgian border.

We travelled by train as far as Beek. There German soldiers were on duty in the station randomly checking travellers. They didn't stop us or question us.

We walked from Beek towards the Belgian border. We had studied our maps, but they weren't precise: we couldn't tell where the German garrisons were. Holland and Belgium were both occupied by the Germans so the line between them wasn't fixed at the time. Dutch and Belgian police controlled a few border points, but the border didn't really exist according to the Germans who passed back and forth without formalities.

We crossed the border that evening. Some tricky moments transpired when the Belgian police grew suspicious of us, but we managed to worm our way through and enter Belgium.

From Hasselt we rode on a series of inter-city streetcars to Brussels. The next day we arrived at Piefke's uncle's home.

His uncle was quite well off. He lived in a villa in a quiet suburb of Brussels. We met several of his neighbours and friends including a fine Austrian couple; the man was a Jew, his wife wasn't. They'd escaped from Austria in 1938 when the Germans overran it and were living in the centre of Brussels near the famous little fountain called the *Manekin Pis*.

CHAPTER XI
NAME CHANGED TO JAN VAN CAPELLE

We stayed with Piefke's uncle while he helped us to acquire important documents. We bought Belgian identification cards through a contact he had in the underground: each card cost three thousand Belgian francs. My picture was attached to my card and then the official stamp of a Belgian town was impressed on it.

I had to give myself a Belgian name. Since soccer was one of my passionate interests and the national teams of Belgium and Germany played against each other every year or two, I knew of an outstanding fullback on the Belgian national team by the name of Jan Van Capelle. His was the only Belgian name I knew so I christened myself Jan Van Capelle.

I filled in the card myself. I invented the address *Chaussée de Bruxelles* (Brussels Road), reasoning that every Belgian city must have a road leading to and from the capital Brussels and designated so. The card was stamped with the authentic seal of Wavre, a city south of Brussels in the Walloon region of Belgium.

So I fabricated my own name and street but the city wasn't chosen by me. A member of the Belgian underground probably worked in the city hall of Wavre or had a contact there with access to official stamps.

Like me, Piefke invented a Belgian name and address for himself. His card, also, bore the seal of Wavre.

Both Piefke and I had brought our *tefillin* (phylacteries) with us; we weren't thinking very clearly when we left Holland! We were so devout that we put on phylacteries every morning to recite our prayers; we never thought of discarding them. We carried them with us wherever we went. They were small, square objects; I always had mine in my pocket.

In Brussels Piefke and I realized that we might step into some thorny situations on our way to Switzerland. It wouldn't be wise to have phylacteries found on us: they would give us away immediately. It was imprudent to have taken them with us from Amsterdam but we were inexperienced at the start.

Piefke's uncle refused to store the phylacteries for us: he didn't want them in his house and didn't expect to stay in Brussels much longer. Instead we left them with some non-Jewish neighbours, a respected doctor and his wife.

After this, Piefke and I set off to cross the border into France. We travelled first to the Belgian town called Tournai opposite Lille, a major city in the industrial area of northern France. Many Belgians living in Tournai worked in French industries: they poured into the area in the morning and streamed back home at night. A flood of people always crossed the border at certain hours of the day, especially between seven and eight o'clock in the morning.

We picked up this information in Brussels. We were told that we could cross into France there without difficulty: Germans weren't stationed at that point because it meant little to them—although they controlled that part of France, too.

Piefke and I mingled with the crowd at Tournai and managed to cross the border without being questioned. We arrived in Lille and strolled around breathing with relief. We began to prepare our next move which was to try to board a train for the city of Nancy.

At the railway station in Lille we were stopped by the Germans. They asked to see our papers. They were checking routinely for irregularities and to find resistance fighters.

They looked at my identity card and let me go. Piefke was arrested. Suddenly I was alone. I didn't know what to do. I thought, "I've lost my companion! Here I am in Lille; I don't know anybody. I'm all by myself. I don't know what to do!"

I decided to move on, to keep going. I dragged myself onto the train and rode until the first stop—a town called Denain.

I got off the train at Denain. I asked for a room at an hotel near the station and spent the night there.

Next morning I was still mulling over the situation. I was shocked, disoriented; I couldn't collect my thoughts.

One train a day covered the distance from Lille to Nancy. I spent the day and another night in Denain and by morning had decided to continue on my way. I walked into the railway station and the first person I saw on the train from Lille was Piefke! I looked up and stared at his face.

I had found him again; we had found each other. Somehow he had wriggled out of detention; he had talked himself out of it. I was indescribably happy to see him. The two of us continued our journey from that little town and arrived in Nancy in the evening.

Nancy is a rather large city. We wandered from the train station toward a business district and, by chance, stumbled on a synagogue close to the station. German soldiers and Gestapo were passing by the building almost casually.

Piefke and I entered the synagogue and joined the men at evening prayers. The rabbi was elderly and dignified, and the men were formal and patrician. The Jewish community of Nancy dated back more than a thousand years.

When the service ended, the men huddled together talking privately in small groups. They sauntered outdoors to the courtyard; we followed them. We had joined them thinking they might be of help to us, but they ignored us.

Then we noticed that we were the only ones without the yellow star. Our accents, even in Hebrew prayers, were unmistakably German. German soldiers and Gestapo were parading on the street nearby with a clear view into the courtyard, so these French Jews must have been bewildered by us; we must have raised their anxiety. They probably worried about who we were and why we were there. And for two people bent on hiding our Jewishness—we had certainly strolled through the wrong door! We exposed our Jewishness by being there. German patrols marching by could have seized us summarily.

Piefke and I glanced at each other apprehensively and quietly left the courtyard. We slipped into the back streets of Nancy, skirting the main parks and squares, and lost ourselves in the city.

It was growing late and we were hungry. We couldn't buy food, it was rationed and sold only with *timbres* (stamps, tickets). We had no ration tickets.

We lit upon a system then that we used frequently afterwards. We entered the cathedral in Nancy and found our way to the confession booths. Piefke sat in one, I in another. We told the priest, "*Nous sommes des Juifs, mon copain et moi. Nous sommes des réfugiés de la Hollande. Nous avons besoin d'aide. Pouvez-vous, voulez-vous nous aider? Nous voulons entrer en Suisse. Voulez-vous nous donner d'assistance?*" (We are Jews, my pal and I. We are refugees from Holland. We need help. Can you, will you help us? We want to get to Switzerland. Will you give us some assistance?)

Piefke or I said words like these in many churches later on; it became one of our main survival techniques. It always brought us at least a meal.

The priest in Nancy was a young man, very sympathetic to us. He offered us a meal of bread and cheese, then advised us to travel via Besançon and to visit the Archbishop there. He would help us with further directions. Besançon is close to the border, with many possible routes branching out to Switzerland.

We pressed on from Nancy. There were few trains: schedules had shrunk and the trains operating were full of German soldiers. It was hard to find a seat or even to get on to a train.

We moved on towards Belfort where we had to change trains. Luck, alertness, and caution each played a part in our reaching Belfort and beyond because the station was packed with Germans. Our hearts pounding we plowed on, arriving in Besançon a day or two later.

Once there, we followed the priest's advice, making our way through narrow ancient streets to the cathedral. The Archbishop's palace stood opposite. We rang the bell at the gate; an old lady came out and asked what we wanted. We answered that we had been sent to the Archbishop by the priest in Nancy.

The Archbishop received us in his office. We explained who we were and why we had come. He told us to sit down, then ordered his housekeeper to prepare a meal for us.

Our aim was entry into Switzerland, so we asked the Archbishop if he had information about conditions at the border. Besançon is approximately eighty kilometres (fifty miles) from the Swiss border but, officially, travel was nil at the time: there was no transportation system between France and Switzerland.

The border was tightly sealed.

The Archbishop gave us some specific directions. He told us to continue forward to a small town called Maîche near the Doubs River which etches the border between France and Switzerland; he recommended that we cross the frontier somewhere along that stretch of the river. After reaching the Swiss side, he advised that we head for a city named La Chaux-de-Fonds in canton Neuchâtel north of Lausanne.

A short time later, we started on a long trek from Besançon: we hiked through rocky meadows, pastureland, and over forested hills. At one juncture we met a group of people led by a guide; they were Jews. We stuck close to them, following them, which vexed the group and guide no end. Hurling threats and insults at us, they tried to shake us off and finally succeeded.

We then reverted to our former procedure. In the rolling foothills of the Jura Mountains the skyline of every village is dominated by a tall church tower or steeple; we moved forward from church to church. We were fed by the priests, and gathered information and directions from them. We advanced steadily this way.

Within a week, we arrived at Maîche. For almost two weeks after that we scouted around the border at the Doubs River, trying to find a safe way across. The border was heavily patrolled: we saw German sentries pacing with guard dogs on footpaths along the cliffs beside the river.

Switzerland was one of the few neutral countries in western Europe. The German forces were on constant alert for spies and smugglers and other illegal traffic attempting to cross the frontier. We knew that crossing it wasn't going to be easy: it was the most heavily guarded border in all Europe.

The only food we ate was fruit we stole from trees on farms close to the border. Our stomachs ached with hunger. We hid and slept in the fields and woods. We moved around mainly at night because movement was dangerous in daytime. The whole area was crawling with German patrols.

We were in the Jura Mountains where the Doubs River runs through a steep narrow gorge. Rocky bluffs covered with tall trees drop abruptly to the water; in spots a fringe of beach emerges beside the water. The channel of the river along this strip is not very wide but the water is deep and swift. On one side is France; on the other, Switzerland.

We came to the top of a mountain on the French side. Perched above the river was an ancient village called Fournet Blancherouche. In the church we found an old priest.

We told the priest that we were *Juifs* (Jews). He cried out, "*Vous êtes des anges, des anges.*" (You are angels, angels). He reacted as though he had never seen Jews before, as though we had stepped right out of the Bible.

He brought out a large bar of chocolate that he had been saving for a long time; I had never seen chocolate like it. He gave it to us and we sat down to a wonderful treat.

Then, demonstrating some worldly sense, he pointed out a house in the village and warned us that Germans were staying there. He described the route we should follow.

Somehow we lost our way. Perhaps his directions were wrong—sometimes our amateur guides didn't know the way well themselves—or maybe in our excitement we missed a turn. Whatever the reason, the path we took was full of patrols with police dogs.

CHAPTER XII
ENTERING SWITZERLAND

It took us about half a day to work our way agonizingly down the mountainside, through the trees and underbrush, to the Doubs River. As much as possible, we tried not to slide down so as not to tear our pants or ruin our clothes.

We reached the riverside. No patrols were about. We could cross, but the river was quite wild and I couldn't swim. Piefke jumped in and swam across. I thought maybe I would be able to swim, maybe fear would force me to swim.

I jumped in the water but I still couldn't swim; I almost drowned. Clutching at some reeds, I managed to keep myself afloat and pull myself out of the water.

I was still on the French side. Piefke was already on the other side and called out to me. I thought, "Holy God, I'm going to be caught here." The patrols would be coming by soon; I could hear the police dogs barking.

I scurried around and saw a boat chained to a metal stake on the bank. Could I tear the chain free or pull the stake out of the ground? Could I tear the boat loose? I had no tools, no equipment. I tore at the chain and pulled and tugged. I kept on pulling, tearing, straining. Almost anything is possible in extremity. I tore the stake out of the ground.

The boat was loose but there were no oars in it. I jumped in and paddled with my hands. It was very awkward; I could scarcely control the boat.

By sheer luck—good luck in bad luck—I maneuvered the boat into the middle of the river. At that point I stood up and heaved myself out. In one leap I almost reached the other side. I scrambled to my feet and waded the rest of the way.

I was on the Swiss side and began to climb the slope. I didn't see Piefke; I had completely lost sight of him. It was growing dark and there were dense woods by the riverside.

I had barely made it to the Swiss side before I heard

German voices on the other. They were shouting that the boat was gone, their patrol boat was gone. They hollered, "*Wo ist das Boot? Das Ruderboot ist verschwunden. Etwas stimmt nicht.*" (Where's the boat? The rowboat is loose. Something's wrong).

The dogs were barking fiercely—I thought they were going to cross the river. It was rumoured that German patrols sometimes crossed to the Swiss side to pick up whoever they were after: the Swiss weren't guarding the border diligently. I didn't see any Swiss guards at all. The Germans didn't come across.

In the morning I met Piefke high up on the hill. When we reached the top together, we lay down in the sun to dry our clothes; we were soaked through.

We hugged and congratulated each other on our accomplishment. "We've done it. We're free. We're in a free country. We've put those miseries behind us."

We had succeeded beyond our wildest dreams. Together we had managed to enter Switzerland in 1942 without any money and without a guide. We had crossed three borders in about six weeks, a remarkable feat considering we had done everything more or less on our own.

Our next objective was La Chaux-de-Fonds. There we would search out the rabbi or some Jewish people and ask them to help us.

We resumed our journey. The region was full of trees and tangled undergrowth; our pants became torn and ragged from tramping through the bush.

We reached an isolated farm. The farmer was working in the field. We spoke to him in French: we asked him the way to La Chaux-de-Fonds and how far it was. He pointed to a road winding down the mountains and a town far ahead in the valley. Then he said to us, "They're very strict with people who come across the border. They're arresting everyone. They don't want any refugees. I want nothing to do with you guys. I can't help you. You'd better get out of here. Go on. Go. And don't tell anyone you saw me."

We told him that we didn't want his help, we didn't want anything from him. We were surprised by what he had said. We thought the isolation had affected his brain or detached him from reality. We were sure he was exaggerating. The Swiss in general would welcome us with open arms. Even if we were arrested, so what? We didn't mind being arrested by the Swiss; they wouldn't do us any serious harm.

From our crossing point at the Doubs River it took us three days to reach La Chaux-de-Fonds. By that time we were tattered, rumpled, and dirty. We looked like bums.

We arrived in La Chaux-de-Fonds in the afternoon. It was a small attractive city. Not knowing if any Jews were living there, the first thing I planned to do was find a telephone booth and look up Jewish names like Cohen and Levy. We walked down the main avenue. Suddenly a man in civilian clothes approached us and said, "*Police secrète suisse. Carte d'identité.*" (Swiss Secret Police. Your identity card).

It was three o'clock in the afternoon. The policeman arrested us and took us to the cantonal jail. It seemed like paradise to us; it was new and clean and warm. We had been outdoors for weeks sleeping in forests and fields.

We were put in a cell with two cots. Everything was neat and scrubbed. We felt very comfortable there after so many weeks on the road.

At six o'clock we were brought some food—hot black coffee and bread; it tasted delicious. We hadn't eaten properly for a long time: we'd been stealing apples from trees. This simple food was excellent.

In the evening, at about eight o'clock, a policeman brought us to an office where there were other police. They began to interrogate us. The questioning went on for a couple of hours.

We weren't searched or told to empty our pockets. Although carrying Belgian identity cards, we didn't use them. We told the Swiss police that we were Jews from Holland: Piefke and I had decided that it would be to our disadvantage if we said we were German Jews. We thought we'd have a better chance of being accepted into Switzerland as Dutch Jews.

We told them we had come all the way from Holland, mostly on foot. We had crossed several borders, including the one into Switzerland.

They wrote down everything we said. Then they went to the phone a few times, calling Bern to ask for instructions.

Eventually, at about ten o'clock, they told us, "There are too many Jews in Switzerland; we can't take any more. If we take any more, Switzerland will be overrun by Jews." This was August 1942. They said, "If we let you stay, there'll soon be more Jews here than Swiss. It can't go on like this. We're very sorry but you can't stay in Switzerland. You have to go back."

They had decided to expel us. This was the directive from Bern.

It was a terrible shock to us. After all our efforts to get there and the safety it meant to us, the decision was catastrophic.

The greatest insult of all was that we had to sign a statement declaring that we understood that, if we ever set foot on Swiss soil again, we would be handed over to the Gestapo at the border. "This time," the Swiss police said, "we'll do you a favor. We'll bring you to the border at an unguarded point. We'll set you free. We'll let you run across to try your luck somewhere else."

There were tears in Piefke's eyes; he was crying. I didn't cry. At that juncture, I became very angry. I accused the police, "*Vous êtes des assassins.* You're murderers. You've condemned us to death and you pretend it isn't so. We can't go back again; we had so much trouble getting here. You can't send us back."

They didn't stir. It didn't upset them a bit to be called murderers. Their decision didn't change.

Then three or four brawny policeman walked in. They told us to stand up. They led us outside and pushed us into a car. Three of them climbed in with us.

It was after ten o'clock on a moonlit night. We drove to a clearing near a place called Le Locle. The car stopped and we were hustled out.

A policeman carrying two loaves of bread gave one to Piefke and one to me. Then he said to us, "This is the border. Go. That's the way, in that direction. Keep on going, keep going. And never come back again."

CHAPTER XIII
BACK TO FRANCE

The border point was riddled with snares and traps. There was a Swiss zone, a neutral zone, then a German zone.

We edged forward through different zones. Suddenly the Germans were shooting at us. We dodged and tried to run for cover. We were separated. I lost Piefke. I don't know what happened to him. We were never together again.

Next morning a farmer driving down the road on his wagon gave me a lift to a town called Morteau. From there I took a train back to Besançon.

I walked from the station down to the Doubs River which winds through this part of France and the city of Besançon. Then I called on the Archbishop again.

He recognized me at once. He said, "I know where you can smuggle yourself into *France Libre*" (Free France). The border between the two parts of France was close to Besançon. "If you can penetrate into *France Libre*, you could go on to Lyon. In Lyon, who knows what may happen?"

Near Besançon there is a town named Arbois where a railroad track constituted the border between the two regions. Many people crossed there, according to the Archbishop, because the Germans weren't guarding as closely at that point.

On a sunny afternoon just after the middle of August I left Besançon by bus on my way to Arbois. Driving through rolling, hilly countryside covered with forests and fields, we passed through villages on the Doubs River; at least once we crossed the river itself. As we were descending the mountainsides into the valleys, a church steeple was conspicuous in the distance.

About two hours later the bus arrived at the outskirts of Arbois. Grapevines covered the hillsides. As we entered the town, a church tower came into view.

Then, startled, I noticed that the town was crowded with Germans. Arbois was virtually an encampment of the German Army! Apparently the Germans had begun to plug the hole in the dam on precisely that day or that week in order to stop the exodus of French people from *France Occupée* (Occupied France). The Archbishop hadn't known about this development.

The bus stopped at the terminus. German soldiers were standing watching everyone who dismounted.

I decided, "I can't walk out the front door." Instead I opened a window and jumped out. Then I hurried away from the bus and disappeared from the depot as fast as I could.

I was in a dangerous position. The whole place was full of Germans; they were patrolling the streets and squares and standing at every corner. It was impossible to avoid them.

I managed to slip into a church near the city hall in the centre of Arbois. I talked to the priest. I said to him, "Can you help me? I have to cross over to the other side."

"Oh," he lamented, "*Vous êtes un malheureux, vous êtes un malheureux.*" (You're an unlucky one, you're an unlucky one). He continued, "You have come to the worst spot in France You won't find a crack in that line now. The Germans have sealed it tight. There's no way to get across."

He gave me no hope and no help. He took me up to his rooms under the roof of a tall building behind the church and, pointing down, he said, "You see, that's the jail. It's full of refugees. They were all caught here. " I looked down at a courtyard enclosed by high walls.

I had to flee from this vicinity: I thought I'd be arrested right there or that he'd turn me in. He was absolutely terrified. Even to talk to me or to harbour me in his rooms frightened him.

I said to him, "Show me the direction. Which way do I go?" He answered, "You see the railroad track there?" He pointed toward *la gare* (the railway station) a few streets away: the track ran behind, at the edge of open fields. There were hills beyond, in the near and far distance. He declared, "You have to cross that track to be in France Libre. That's the border."

I thought, "It's not very far, just a few hundred metres away." German soldiers were patrolling the track. I would try to cross early in the morning; I figured there wouldn't be many guards on duty then.

I skittered through the town toward the railway station and stole into a garden near by. Sunflowers and other tall big-leaved plants were growing in the garden; I crouched among them and lay down to sleep.

During the night a violent storm blew up. The rain beat down. I tried to shield myself with flowers but they didn't cover me: they grew heavy with rain, drooped and dripped on me. Soon I was completely drenched.

I waited until daylight, then forced myself up. Hurrying from the garden, I made for the railroad track. Suddenly four uniformed Germans were blocking my way with police dogs.

They arrested me. I acknowledged that I intended to go to *France Libre*; I saw no point in denying it.

I did not really want to go to *France Libre*, because I sensed that it would not go well for me there, either. Maybe this feeling had come over me because the Swiss had driven me out; I had never expected that; it had thrown me off balance. Then Piefke had vanished. After that the Archbishop and the priest had let me down. Worse still, I had made the same mistake in Arbois that I'd made in Switzerland: Piefke and I had attracted attention in Switzerland by walking into La Chaux-de-Fonds in daytime. I should have tried to leave Arbois during the storm at night. I don't know why I didn't. Waiting until morning was a serious mistake; that was how I got caught. After such blunders, shocking turns and misguidance, I could have lost the strength to survive.

CHAPTER XIV
JAIL IN FRANCE AND BELGIUM

I was put in the jail in Arbois. It was a small, old, dilapidated place. As the priest had said, there were lots of others.

The German *Geheime Feldpolizei*, which was a military branch of the Gestapo, came and questioned me. That's when I invented my story.

I said I was Belgian and the situation in Belgium was tough; there was no way I could get by in Belgium. My parents were dead; but I had a brother. My brother was living in Lyon. He had a milk business; he was selling milk in Lyon and needed somebody to deliver it. So I was on my way to Lyon to be with my brother and help him deliver milk.

That's what I told the German police. They sentenced me to three months in jail for attempting to cross the border. Three months in jail in Arbois. After that I would be sent back to Belgium to verify my identity card and confirm that I was who I said I was.

I stayed in jail in Arbois for three months. Lice were the biggest problem there—the jail was swarming with them. I had never had lice before but I became infested: the mattresses were full of them so they spread everywhere.

I had lice in my hair; I could feel them crawling. Whenever I touched my hair, I would pull out lice and crack them between my fingers. They pop as their body breaks.

They were all over me, even in my armpits and pubic hair: wherever there was hair on my body, lice were in it. I washed myself scrupulously, but the jail was so full of lice that I couldn't get rid of them.

My circumcision made me apprehensive; I was afraid it might be noticed in jail. It was a detail I had to keep in mind. Though other men were circumcised, too, not only Jews, I wanted to avoid suspicion or questions about it.

Some of the prisoners in the Arbois jail were criminals, but everyone there had been arrested for trying to cross into Free France. When my three-month sentence was over, I was started on my way back to Belgium.

The transfer was done in stages. First I was sent to Besançon. In Besançon there's a vast and formidable *Maison d'Arrêt*, a prison situated on a butte above the old city. It's a classic prison with cell blocks radiating from a central tower and high walls surrounding the complex. Some wings were used by the French; others were partitioned for use by the Germans. Prisoner transports were assembled there.

I spent three weeks in solitary confinement in Besançon: I don't know why suddenly I was put into solitary. The food was vile: it was minimal in all Gestapo jails. I was handed a hunk of dry bread in the morning and watery soup three times a day: their bread was baked with sawdust to give it weight and the soup was a thin broth with a few vegetables floating in it.

I was starving all the time. But I treasured my hunk of bread for many hours: I would look at it and touch it all day long; then I ate it slowly at night. This was the only way I could sleep through the night. Otherwise hunger would keep me awake.

I lost a near fatal amount of weight at this time. I was weighed in Besançon: I weighed 92 pounds (41 kilograms). Before that, I had weighed about 135 pounds (60 kilograms). For my height of five feet eight inches (174 centimetres), I had become extremely thin.

From Besançon I was transferred to Dijon. As I walked into the jail an SS man rushed at me, screaming, "*Sind Sie Jude? Sind Sie Jude?*" (Are you a Jew? Are you a Jew?) I looked him in the eye and said, "*Nein.*" (No). I answered him so coolly that he didn't question or examine me further.

The Dijon jail must have been the worst jail in France. It was a gloomy, medieval place. Inmates were treated very harshly. We weren't treated like Jews—which would have been worse; supposedly we were Belgians, so we were treated as Belgians. Yet the guards beat us prisoners constantly.

After a week, a transport was assembled for Belgium. We were put on an ordinary train in special cars guarded by German soldiers and German police.

There was one guard for every two prisoners. Prisoners weren't handcuffed but, wherever we went, even to the toilet, a German guard went with us.

It was a slow train and quite a long trip. A number of times I thought of leaping from a toilet window or opening a compartment door and jumping out. But the Germans were watching so closely that there wasn't much chance of doing it.

I was thinking continually about escaping and tried to develop a plan. Several times I thought, "I should do something now; I should make a run for it." But I didn't take the step.

We arrived in Lille in the evening where we had to change trains for Brussels. We were herded off the train, then led from one platform to another when, suddenly, a guy who I suspected was Jewish disappeared. I saw him going. The station was so crowded with people that he vanished into the throng; the Germans couldn't follow and lost him. He slipped away in Lille.

I told myself, "That guy did the right thing. I should do that, too." I tried to figure out how to do it, how to do it. I looked for an opportunity, but opportunities were limited.

Then we boarded the train for Brussels. Still I kept thinking, "Should I jump?" If I went through to Brussels with a false identity card, I was a doomed man. I thought, "The only chance I have is to break free."

For one reason or another, I didn't jump; I didn't run. There were few chances to do so, but sometimes we have to make our own chances. Even so I didn't do anything.

We pulled into Brussels and were lugged away to St. Gilles jail. It was the worst jail I had been in yet: about three thousand political prisoners were incarcerated there; I could hear continuous barking and screaming. It was a hellish place.

I was locked in a cell and kept there for about a week. Then I was summoned for interrogation with some other prisoners.

We were led to a large room partitioned into separate cubicles. In each one an SS man presided at a table.

I realized I had to make a good impression, to give the appearance that I was telling the truth. A booth became empty; my turn was next. The interrogator in that booth was an older man who looked experienced. I was sure he would see through me fast so I held back to try to avoid him.

In a moment another booth was free. The interrogator there was a youth of eighteen or nineteen. I thrust myself in with him.

I told him my story. As usual I had to play a strange game: I purported to be a Belgian but my name wasn't Wallon, French Belgian, it was Flemish; and I couldn't speak Flemish. I could speak Dutch but not Flemish which is Belgian Dutch and somewhat different from the language spoken in Holland. So I always spoke to the Germans in broken German to forestall their calling an interpreter who would have realized immediately that I wasn't who I said I was.

I talked to this young SS man in broken German. I told him about my brother and the milk business in Lyon. Then I watched as he wrote, '*Der Angeklagte macht einen glaubenswürtigen Eindruck*' (the accused gives the impression that he is telling the truth). After that, I was hurried back to my cell.

We always had to move rapidly. We were wakened at St. Gilles at five o'clock in the morning and then did absolutely nothing. We were given almost nothing to eat. I was dangerously thin: it surprised me that I didn't catch tuberculosis or some other wasting disease.

Again I sat in jail in filthy conditions. St. Gilles was full of lice like the French jails. I thought, "I'll never get out of this hole."

I had almost given up hope. Prisoners were shot every night in the courtyard; I could hear the shots and screams.

If the Gestapo discovered that someone was a Jew, they shot the person immediately. I thought, "They'll come at any moment; they'll discover I'm a Jew because my identity card is false. How can Wavre confirm that I'm Jan Van Capelle, that I used to live there? The address probably doesn't exist. The name with my personal statistics certainly doesn't exist."

One day, about two weeks after I arrived there, the *Feldwebel* (sergeant) appeared and shouted, "Van Capelle!" I said to myself, "This is it, the day of reckoning."

I sat, hesitating. The sergeant snapped, "Come out! Fast!" Everything had to be done in quick time.

He ordered, "Take your stuff!"

I said to myself, "Oh, no. It's over."

He shrilled, "Why don't you come faster? You're free!"

I said, "What?" I couldn't believe it. Free! How could I be free? Free!

I didn't believe him. Free! Impossible. But I couldn't reveal what I thought.

Then the process of freeing me started. It took six hours until I'd gone round to all the different offices and officials and been checked and signed out and released through all those doors, doors, doors.

And there I was one evening at the end of December, 1942, a free man in Brussels. A German Jew. Via Holland. Via Switzerland. Via France. I was free in Brussels!

I didn't know anyone. I had never lived in Belgium. A war was on. What was I supposed to do now?

CHAPTER XV
BRUSSELS 1943

When the Germans set me free from St. Gilles, they gave me a warning and a letter of instruction: I was to report to the police chief in Wavre within twenty-four hours. If I failed to report in Wavre, I would be arrested again.

But I couldn't report to Wavre. It was just a dot on the map to me. I had never been there. I knew that, even without civil records and official inquiries, the police chief would easily discover that my identity was false. I decided I'd better get out of Brussels or disappear underground.

Another prisoner had been released from St. Gilles at the same time as I was. He was going to the Gare du Nord, a train station in Brussels, to take a train home. So I tagged along with him.

On the way I noticed a Salvation Army hostel near the *Gare du Nord*. When we reached the station, I said good-bye to the other fellow.

It had grown quite dark by this time. Retracing my steps, I went to the Salvation Army hostel. The officers received me: they took me in. They gave me a bowl of soup and told me I could sleep there for one night.

The following day I walked around Brussels wondering what to do next. All kinds of schemes entered my head.

I thought of finding some Jews. I saw a man on the street who I thought was a Jew; I followed him. He tried to avoid me but I collared him. Shoving him into a corner, I grabbed him by the throat and said, "I know that you're a Jew; don't deny it. I'm a Jew, too. I want you to help me. You have to give me shelter or tell me where to find other Jews. I'm here alone. I don't know anybody."

He was scared. He tried to shake me off. Finally he gave me an address and told me how to get there.

I arrived at the address and discovered the offices of the Jewish Council. I went in. The people there told me the situation in Brussels was desperate for Jews and the only thing to do was give myself up. Again that was the advice I received-surrender to the Germans!

I realized that I was in a trap. I escaped from the spot as fast as I could. Luckily I got away; the Germans could have been watching the place.

I decided then that I would never again have anything to do with the Jewish Councils. I would never go near them again. I would never appeal to them for help. I wanted nothing to do with them. I wanted nothing from them.

Then I remembered the Austrian couple I had met through Piefke's uncle. Piefke and I had been to the flat where the couple lived. So, racking my memory, I traced my way to the statue of *Manneken Pis* and, and from there I managed to find the flat, which was close by.

The woman remembered me; she was very friendly and kind. Her husband had been arrested by the Gestapo but she was in a fairly safe position: she had a German passport because Hitler had annexed Austria in 1938. As a German and a gentile, she wasn't under suspicion.

In reality this woman was active in the Belgian underground. That night she took me to stay at another flat. Then she spread the word about me to others in the resistance. I was shuffled from one flat to another for several nights.

A few days later I decided to venture outside Brussels to the suburb where Piefke's uncle lived. I wanted to try to locate him and maybe Piefke.

The uncle wasn't there any more and the neighbors had no news of him or Piefke. They recognized me and were pleased to see me. They invited me into their house.

I had left my phylacteries with them. The woman said to me, "Are you back again?" Right away she went to a cupboard and returned soon saying, "Here. Here are your holy objects." She didn't know what to call them. "Here they are," she said. "Do you want to take them with you?"

I said, "No; thanks very much. I can't take them with me. I don't know where I'm going."

The people I was staying with in Brussels were all in the Belgian resistance movement called the *Armée Blanche*. At first they were suspicious of me; they thought I might be a spy. I told them that I wasn't really Jan Van Capelle, though I used that name. I said my real name was Eli Hart and that I was Dutch.

The Austrian woman accepted me for what I said I was since she'd met me under that name when I had first come from Holland. Then, quizzing me themselves, the others became very interested in me after I told them about my Swiss and other jail experiences. They wanted people like me to join the underground army to do illegal work and sabotage.

They talked to me and induced me to join them. "After a while," they emphasized, "all of us will go to England to be trained as commandos for the eventual invasion of Europe." This prospect appealed to me: I was longing to become a fighter of some sort. Connected with them, I could look forward to serving in the regular British army, the commandos or some other force, and fighting the Nazis in the open.

Therefore I attached myself to the *Armée Blanche*; it seemed the only way to sustain myself. There were few means of surviving unless one was part of an organization.

In Brussels our group always met on the Rue Verte near the Gare du Nord. A slummy, red light district with a floating sea of unsavory types and questionable enterprises. It was the least conspicuous place for the underground to meet.

Our group organized and carried out raids and attacks, particularly to obtain ration tickets. Everybody had to have ration tickets and most underground people didn't have them. One couldn't buy basic foods without stamps.

We stole the stamps from the administrative offices that issued them. We would rush in waving pistols and demand all the tickets. We had to rush in suddenly, move quickly, and get away fast. We did it in the daytime when the offices were open.

We were armed with pistols to show force but we didn't use force unless we had to. The people we confronted usually knew they couldn't resist us successfully so they handed over the tickets without commotion. Some officials actually co-operated with us; they were probably in sympathy with our cause. Others tried to resist.

Sometimes there were German guards on duty at the locations. We tried to avoid meeting them: either we struck when they weren't around or sneaked in and out through a back or side door so they wouldn't detect us.

We also set explosives at bridges, tunnels, and railroad overpasses: the purpose was to stop the German movement of ammunition and soldiers. One of our main functions was to disrupt the transportation system.

I teamed up with fellows who were experts in explosives; some were engineers. Most often I acted as a lookout for them; they did the skilled work that I wasn't trained to do. My job was to guard them, alert them, and cover their retreat.

These sorties were offensive attacks. We tried to do the utmost damage to the Germans and were ready to shoot if we were in danger.

At times we had to use our pistols. That made us especially vulnerable because the Germans were equipped with superior weapons. Shooting was our last resort.

Sometimes we ambushed and shot at German staff cars to try and kill specific officers. It was difficult to know how many we hit because we had to escape from the scene quickly. I was always ready, however, to fire another shot to make sure we completed our mission.

These activities all took place in Brussels or close to it. Brussels is a broad metropolitan area made up of many distinct districts. After a while we reduced the amount of railway sabotage we did because the Germans retaliated by executing disproportionate numbers of local people. This was too high a price to pay.

After a couple of months our group of fifteen had become a hot target. In late February 1943 the leaders decided to ship us out to England.

We gathered one evening in the basement of a house on the Rue Verte. We were about to leave Brussels in order to fly to England. We were celebrating our departure: that night we were to drive to a place near Antwerp where a plane would land, pick us up, and transport us to England.

I'd spent all my Belgian money that afternoon. There wasn't much one could buy in those days so I bought some silly things just to get rid of it. I thought I'd be in England the next day; I wouldn't need Belgian money any more.

I'd developed the habit of studying every building I went into to devise ways of leaving it: I'd learned that it was often easy to enter an establishment but quite difficult to get out, especially to get out fast. The house we were assembled in that night was one I'd been scrutinizing for some time.

We were enjoying the party, happy and optimistic about our move; we ate and drank wine, toasting the group. Our leader, a French officer, was with us. Among us were Russians and other eastern Europeans who had escaped from prisoner-of-war camps or deserted the Axis troops. We were all shipping out together.

Suddenly we heard German boots stamping down the steps. Stamp Stamp Stamp. Storming the basement door. Shots were fired through the door.

The moment I heard boots, I jumped straight up. I knew that sound, its meaning: get out or be shot. We would all be dead.

I rushed up the inside stairs of the house as the Germans burst through the basement door. The place rattled with gun-fire. The Germans had machine-guns and heavy ammunition; we had only small pistols to fight them off.

The building we were in was three or four stories high. I raced to the top floor as fast as I could.

I knew there was a ledge outside a window—it was the top of a small wall jutting into a courtyard. I thought, "I'll sit near the window. If they come after me, I'll get out and hide on the ledge."

All this took only a few minutes. There was continuous shooting. Then the boots started up the stairs. They stomped into every room.

I clambered out on the ledge. Figures appeared at the window and shone strong lights everywhere. They spotted me. They yelled, "*Gib auf!*" (Surrender).

The moment I heard that, I jumped. I didn't know where I would land. The ledge was three or four stories high; I dropped from there to the courtyard.

In European cities the interior courtyards surrounded by buildings and walls are paved with brick or stone. I could have broken my back or legs on the pavement or seriously injured myself; at the moment I didn't feel anything.

I had little time to think. A German came out on the ledge right after I jumped. He shone a flashlight on me and started to shoot.

There were several doors leading into the courtyard. I thought, "I'll run for a door and try it. If it opens, I'll be able to get away; if it's locked, I'm trapped, cornered."

The German was shooting and shooting and shooting. I scurried towards a door and pushed hard. It opened.

I fled through the door into a house. I was in a dark hallway. I ran to the other end. I thought, "I'd better get out of here. They may surround the area; maybe it's surrounded already."

I opened the front door and stepped onto a street opposite the Rue Verte. I kept on going, going, going. Then I saw a streetcar and jumped on board. After a few stops I transferred to another streetcar going in a different direction. I did this several times until I was far from the Rue Verte.

I thought maybe I had been hit somewhere. I was wearing a beret; I removed it. There were five bullet holes in it but I wasn't hit. The closest call that I'd had for some time and I wasn't hurt.

I went to see the Austrian woman again. I told her what had happened.

People are often betrayed; it was common during the war. Someone must have spilled our plans or unwittingly betrayed us. The French captain who led us was frequently involved with prostitutes on the Rue Verte. Some prostitutes acted as informers for the Germans. I was sure that one of them had betrayed us to the Gestapo.

CHAPTER XVI
RETURN TO FARMING

My underground-army career was over. Judgement advised that I couldn't operate effectively in that sphere any more.

I was bent on returning to farming: I'd intended to do so immediately after my release from St. Gilles. Now my Austrian friend concurred. She made inquiries and put me in contact with a Dutchman named Dirk.

Dirk was a painter who'd married a Belgian girl and settled in Belgium. He had the ruddy face and blond hair of Dutchmen depicted in many Flemish and Dutch paintings. He was a burly, jolly, happy-go-lucky man.

When I met him, he offered to help me find a job on a farm. He was living north of Brussels beyond Laeken in an outer suburb called Strombeek-Bever.

One Sunday morning we canvassed the neighborhood farms. Dirk persuaded a farmer and his wife to hire me. So I went to work for them.

I lived with a very poor family; my room cost a trifle yet it was income for these people. I was able to eat on the farm—a major advantage of farm work since I didn't have ration tickets.

The farming was mixed: there were animals and extensive crop land. The farmer was getting rich by selling on the black market. Grain brought high prices there so workers were denied an extra slice of bread.

The farmer's wife was especially niggardly and a slave-driver: she wanted maximum work for a minimum amount of food. In her view the farmhands never worked hard enough and always ate too much. It was a wretched place.

I often visited Dirk. He was always in a cheerful mood: he would laugh and ridicule all the privations. Whenever I came, he offered me a meal; he was extremely generous. Since I didn't have ration tickets, he shared his own rations with me.

Sanitary conditions on the farm were also deplorable; it was foul there. One day my left hand began to swell; it grew larger and larger. I bathed it in hot water and swallowed pills given to me by a farmhand, but with no improvement.

After a while I realized that I had to see a doctor. My hand had become huge and distorted. I appealed to Dirk; his sister-in-law recommended a young doctor in a district close to where I worked.

I went to the doctor and he said, "I have to cut this open right now. If I don't, you may lose your hand. You have blood poisoning."

He made an incision on the back of my left hand between the last two fingers. A gush of blood mixed with pus and dirt spurted out.

With sulfa drugs unavailable, the hand needed slow, painstaking cleansing. Three days of repeated washing went by before the infected matter drained away completely.

After approximately a week, my hand healed. The doctor had operated superbly and I was deeply grateful for what he had done. Without Dirk and his wife and the sister-in-law who directed me to the doctor, I might have lost it. What would I have done then? I doubt that I could have survived the war with only one hand.

Manure must have invaded a pimple or blister and infected it. Working in the stable—a neglected, dirty one—I could not keep my hands clean.

The last two fingers of my left hand did not fully regain their strength. For a while I thought I had lost the ability to milk: milking requires two strong hands-pressure has to be applied equally with both.

I was impeded by my left hand for some time, but slowly I retrained it and the hand recovered its strength.

Apart from this crisis, I was never really sick during the war. I don't remember being sick over a period of four to five years. I always forced myself to feel well; I couldn't afford to be sick.

I continued working on that farm. But when my hand was healed and had regained its strength, I realized that I was fed up with the farmer and his stingy wife.

Furthermore, I was not very welcome at the house where I lived. The people were acting nervous and scared: they let me know every day that I wasn't welcome there. The man was working again in the coal mines near by and my rent was no longer essential for them.

So I decided to take a chance somewhere else. Not much could be gained by staying where I was.

I heard talk of a shortage of farm laborers on the other side of Brussels at Waterloo. So I went there by streetcar.

At that time Waterloo was a quiet, rural town set in rich, rolling farmland. I walked down the main street, Chaussée de Bruxelles, and stopped at a farm called Ferme de Mont St. Jean. I asked for work. No help was needed.

I walked on past the Gendarmerie (Police Station) and stopped at another farm. I asked the farmer if he needed any help. He returned, "You know how to milk?" He led me into the barn and told me, "Sit down and milk."

I sat down; he gave me a pail. He watched as I milked and saw that I milked very well. "Good," he said. "You've got a job."

At that point a job was easy to find in Waterloo because the Germans had picked up many young Belgian men and sent them to work in Germany. There was a serious shortage of farmhands.

The farmer in Waterloo was unable to provide me with a bedroom; I wanted to live on the farm, at least for a while. I suggested to the farmer, "I'll sleep in the stable;" and he agreed.

I slept in the stable for more than six months. Each night I made up my bed of straw in the corner. Sometimes the animals got loose and could have run me over. Though it was precarious in that respect, I soon felt quite comfortable there.

The farmhouse, kitchen garden, and barns were in the centre of Waterloo. The fields were on the edge of town.

Fernand, the farmer, was a young fellow whose father had recently died. He and his elderly mother were running the farm together; they needed a great deal of help.

They kept thirty or forty milking cows. I did all the milking by myself. Sometimes they joined me in cleaning the stables, but they couldn't do this when they had work to do in the fields.

Because I did nothing else, I was able to handle the work by myself. I was happy to work all the time. I couldn't visit Dirk. I couldn't saunter in the streets because of frequent heavily armed German patrols in the district.

My one diversion was going to the movies: I went on Sundays before the afternoon milking. The town cinema was on the main street close to the farm. I saw many French films starring the actresses Danielle Darieux, Edwige Feuillères, and Michele Morgan among others.

The resistance was very evident in the Waterloo area. People were resisting openly; several uprisings occurred. Often there was shooting in the streets.

When I drove the cows out to pasture and brought them back in for milking, I would pass by a house behind the communal administration building which I recognized was used by the resistance. With rebellion so close to the surface, the Germans were massing troops in the locality to subdue the population. It was a very explosive spot.

In Waterloo the lice in my hair were a plague. My hair grew fast in those days and I had to have it cut often. I would sit in the barber's chair thinking, "What if he sees the lice? He'll throw me out." The barber wouldn't tolerate lice on his combs and scissors; nothing worse can infest a barbershop.

I was always on tenterhooks in the shop, especially when the barber was cutting my hair. I thought, "The lice will come out at any moment. I'm covered with them. The barber will notice the nits."

Finally I decided to do something about it. I went to a pharmacy in Waterloo and asked for a remedy for lice. The pharmacist gave me some powder and I used it again and again all over my body.

After a while I seemed to lower the numbers; gradually the lice disappeared. It took a long time to control them because I was sleeping in the stable. I didn't live in sanitary quarters or keep sufficiently clean. I wasn't changing my clothes enough-I couldn't; I didn't have many clothes. These factors all contributed to the problem, yet I managed to overcome it.

I had another stubborn problem at the time. After I moved to Waterloo, a boil developed on my neck. Then I was plagued with boils—large, ugly, painful swellings. They ballooned on my neck and the back of my head.

I had no treatment for boils. I let them ripen until they burst, then squeezed them. Pus poured from them like water.

I had one boil after another, a constant affliction. Even now there are marks on my neck and head where the boils were. People suggested they were associated with my age—young adults are susceptible to skin eruption. But the boils were unusually severe so I'm inclined to think they were related to either poor hygiene or malnutrition.

In Waterloo I walked through town with the cattle every day, driving them from the stable to the pasture and from the pasture back to the stable. The Germans had set up posts to check everybody but they never questioned me. Time and time again I went through their check posts and they didn't ask me anything. I was Jean, Jan Van Capelle, *vacher* (cowherder). I was so shabbily dressed and insignificant-looking that the Germans never stopped me.

I didn't tell anyone in Waterloo that I was a Jew. In Strombeek-Bever the people I'd worked for and those I lived with knew I was Jewish. After my experience with them, I stopped identifying myself as a Jew because I'd observed that people were uneasy with me around: knowing I was a Jew made them tense and irritable. It seemed to make them feel guilty. Maybe they were fearful that they themselves would be arrested.

Consequently, I decided that I wasn't going to mention it again. I told nobody; no one in Waterloo knew who I was. It was the best way to proceed. From then on I lost my identity completely. This was April 1943.

I stayed in Waterloo for a long time working extremely hard with never enough to eat. Three slices of bread was the most I was allowed at a meal and I could have eaten six. I compensated for this by milking directly into my mouth; I drank milk straight from the udder. It never made me sick; I may have developed immunity to the bacteria. On the other hand, the boils may have resulted from drinking the milk. But I kept up my strength this way. Though the farmer gave me too little to eat, I took advantage of what was available.

I worked very hard on that farm. In the beginning I thought I wouldn't be able to keep it up, that I couldn't keep on working like that. But I grew accustomed to it.

From what I knew, the Germans had conquered most of Russia by this time and were successful even in Africa. So I couldn't conceive of the war ending with anything other than a German victory.

It seemed to me sometimes that my struggle was all in vain, that I was straining myself to the limit and that I couldn't win. I wasn't optimistic at that point.

What drove me on, however, was the thought of premature death. I decided to do whatever I could to hang on to life. It was my basic motivation: to stay alive as long as I could. One way or another I tried to scramble through, to see if I could escape what the Nazis had decreed for Jews. Yet I didn't really believe I would succeed.

One thing was certain: I was never going to surrender. I was never going to give myself up to be delivered to a concentration camp. This resolve was foremost in my mind. All my effort was aimed at avoiding a concentration camp; it was my main objective. And if ever I had to go to a concentration camp, I was determined to carry at least one dead German on my back.

Fernand, the young farmer in Waterloo, was hoping to get married and took up with several girls. He began to count on having me around: I relieved him of many tasks. He let me plan and follow up my own work on the farm.

Then he married. His wife moved into the house and proved to be much nicer than him or his mother. She saw that I had few clothes so she gave me his old pants and shirts. She was very considerate and tried to help me as much as she could.

I always kept the money I saved with me. I had nowhere to put it— I didn't know of any safe place—so I hid it in a pocket of my jacket or under my pillow at night.

I carried my mother's bracelet on me for several years. I kept it through all the jails without its being discovered. In one jail the Gestapo took my jacket away; when they returned it to me, the bracelet was still in the pocket.

One day in Waterloo the old lady asked me to dig up her vegetable garden. I dug it up and somehow lost the bracelet. Though I looked for it carefully, I couldn't find it. I never found it after that.

In the fall of 1943, there was a bumper crop of sugar beets which had to be dug out of the ground by hand. Crews of contract workers travelled from farm to farm throughout Belgium to bring in the harvest.

A crew came to the farm where I worked. These people worked in the fields for long hours; I would meet them and talk to them at night.

I became friendly with the leader of the crew who asked me in surprise, "Why do you stay in this hole? What are you doing here? It's a miserable job and you never get enough to eat." I had told him about the three slices of bread and he saw it with his own eyes. He said, "They're rotten people. All they want is to make loads of money on the black market." The farm was within easy access to the black-market trade in Brussels.

"What are you staying here for?" he asked. "You get nothing out of it. Why don't you go to Liège in the eastern part of Belgium? You'll find big farms there and nice people. You'll get a good job there; the way you work, you'll get the best job in Belgium! You have nothing to worry about."

I didn't make a move for a while. I thought, "I have no legal papers; it's dangerous for me to move across Belgium. If I go, who knows what might happen? The farmers there might not hire a guy without papers." Since my release from St. Gilles, the identity card was useless: my Belgian alias was probably on a Gestapo list.

Eventually, in October of 1943, I had reached the limit with three slices of bread, unending work, and sleeping in stables. It simply wasn't right. To live like that was almost as demeaning as being in a concentration camp. I thought, "I'm barely surviving. Who knows how much longer this war will last?" I couldn't see an end in sight.

There were employment agencies at the time which placed workers with farmers needing hands. The migrant workers knew an agent in the region near Liège; they had given me his name.

I wrote to the agent. He answered and told me to go to a specific farm.

I decided that I would take the chance and go out there. Maybe I would find a different way of life, improve my situation.

CHAPTER XVII
WORK NEAR LIEGE

I left Waterloo. Over my shoulder I carried a bag like a potato sack with a few clothes in it.

From Brussels I took a train via Louvain. West of Liège I disembarked at the small station of Fexhe-le-Haut-Clocher.

I asked the station-master for directions to the farm. His reply indicated that I was expected there.

I walked a zigzag route from the station through a pretty town of low, red and brown brick buildings. The fields belonging to the farm stretched beyond an old church.

The brick farm buildings were constructed like a fortress. The barns, stables, sheds, and handsome farmhouse formed a quadrangle around an inner courtyard. In the middle of the courtyard lay a large manure pile which strangely enough exuded no smell. Surrounding the buildings, gardens and fields extended to the far distance.

The farm was stocked with horses, cows, and bulls—about forty horses and forty or fifty cows and calves. The farmer was breeding steers and horses and had many young animals. It was very progressive farming.

I was hired by the farmer and immediately given a room in the attic of the farmhouse. It was small with little in it but, at least, it was a room. It was decent, civilized.

I began my work as a milker. Whenever I saw the farmer, Monsieur Roberti, in the first week I was there, I thought that he looked unwell. He was a young man, about thirty-five years of age, with a wife and two children.

The farmer died suddenly at the end of the week. The whole place became unsettled. Farmhands gossiped about whether or not the widow could manage the farm by herself.

I focussed on milking. With Monsieur Roberti gone, I was left alone. The widow, Madeleine, helped me irregularly.

A short time later, her father arrived from Liège. Retired, over sixty years old, he'd been a prosperous farmer, a breeder of horses and bulls. Now, faced with his daughter's predicament, he came out of retirement to take charge of the farm.

Monsieur Degive was a stern-looking man. He had injured a leg and limped.

After a while it became too much for the widow to help with the milking; she had many other things to do. Instead she gave me more responsibility and asked the maid Claire to help me.

Claire wasn't trained so I taught her how to milk and she soon acquired the skill. She helped me every day and especially on Sunday because, on that day, we stopped work early. On weekends when Claire went to visit her parents, the widow helped with Sunday's milking.

Claire was the daughter of Polish immigrants. Her father worked in the mines near Liège. She had grown up in Belgium and spoke fluent French. She had blond hair and a pale, round, Slavic face with broad high cheekbones.

I was a very skilled milker. I had learned from the Friesians, the best milkers in the world, and these Belgian farmers took notice of it; they respected me for my work.

I milked and cleaned the stables. I worked all the time—I never went out. If the farmers were suspicious of my cloistered life, they never talked to me about it.

The old man, Monsieur Degive, became quite interested in me. I was the only worker who stayed overnight; all the others left. Many were married and lived in the village.

At night the farm was a medieval stronghold. The animals were in the stables. A solid, wooden gate closed it off completely.

One day the old man gave me the farm key and told me to open the gate every morning and close it every night. So I became the gatekeeper.

The first thing I observed on this farm was that I could eat as much as I wanted. The part of Belgium around Liège was a rich area; but the farms in Waterloo were productive, too. Here, however, people were much more generous. If they were concerned about the black market, it wasn't obvious to me. Maybe its importance to them was on a large scale, not just to sell a few extra slices of bread or glasses of milk.

The old lady, Madame Degive, sincerely grew to like me. She taught me how to bake bread. Once a week she baked thirty-two enormous round loaves in an outdoor oven. I was the one who always helped her to place the bread on long handles straight into the oven; then I pulled the handles out. I helped her to do this every Friday.

In the evenings I ate with the other farmhands in a room off the kitchen. After they'd eaten and left, the old lady would call me into the kitchen and give me another meal—a better one than the workers ate; it was part of the family's meal.

The old lady would tell me to polish her grandsons' shoes: in this way she allowed me to 'work' for the extra food she gave me. But having me clean the shoes was just a pretext.

Later the boys came to me; they were lively youngsters about eight and ten years of age. I would tell them stories and they were so keen! Every night they ran to me while I polished their shoes; they wanted to hear another story.

I told them stories from the Brothers Grimm, from Wilhelm Busch's Max and Moritz, and from the Bible. Also, I made up stories: I was hard pressed now and then to think up a new one. I noticed that after a while even the old man was listening to my stories.

Sometimes I helped the boys with their schoolwork; perhaps in doing this I revealed too much of myself. I certainly showed that I was more intelligent than I appeared to be and that I wasn't the person I pretended to be. The old man may have talked to his wife about it: he knew there was more to me than first appeared. But no one ever said a word to me about it.

CHAPTER XVIII
MONSIEUR DEGIVE

When I opened the gate in the morning, the old farmer sometimes came out and talked to me. One morning he said, "You know, Jean, I'd like to have your papers. I can clear you from going to Germany. You don't have to go to work there; you can stay here. I have good contacts; I can fix it up completely. Don't worry; I can clear you."

I answered, "Ah..." I began to tell him a tale. "I don't have my papers," I said. "I left them with my uncle in Brussels."

Twice he asked me for my papers, then he gave up. He realized that I had no usable papers. He never mentioned it again. He never asked me about anything.

Monsieur Degive knew that there was something clandestine about me. Puzzled—he took a chance on me.

I established a close relationship with him. He was a very intelligent man and saw some potential in me.

He went out of his way to be kind to me. He tried to teach me skills that he knew well. For instance he asked me if I would like to learn something about horses; he was an experienced horse breeder.

Sometimes we sat up together all night waiting for a mare to foal. A horse's birth is very difficult, especially if the foal comes out legs first. The old man taught me how to pull out the foal, when to pull and when not to pull. His instructions were excellent and I was appreciative.

He detected that I was interested in learning, so he also taught me how to breed bulls. He was a renowned bull-breeder. He said to me, "You have to look for the quality here and quality there. You have to look for this feature and that."

He owned a magnificent bull. Other farmers came to have their cows inseminated by the bull and he put me in charge of this service.

He said, "You're going to handle the bull. I don't want anyone else to control him." So whenever a cow was to be impregnated, I had to run with the bull, lift up the cow's tail, and control the bull.

Other farmhands were afraid of the bull, but the old man told me, "Once the bull knows you, you don't have to worry about him. Don't be frightened of him. He won't do anything to you." And the old man was right; he knew.

With thirty or forty milking cows and many young cattle to care for, I performed a demanding job. Still, the attitude and trust of Monsieur Degive more than compensated me. He did more for me than he was obliged to do in many ways,.

I was much happier there than I'd been on other farms. I was well fed and housed and made to feel like a human being. I worked very hard although not harder than in Waterloo and the treatment I received was better. I could even put my earnings under my mattress and leave them untouched for weeks.

I bantered often with Claire. She was cheerful and bright; she caught on to things fast. However, I didn't want to get involved with any girls—the situation was too unstable—so no intimacy ever developed between us.

These farmers were members of the Catholic church; everyone in the area was Catholic. The priest would visit the farm on his rounds and, when he saw me, asked why I wasn't attending church. The only explanation I could think of was: "I have so much to do; I don't feel like going to church." He asked me once or twice but didn't insist; he didn't hound me.

Some of the other workers asked why I never went to church. Subtle pressures were put on me to become more involved with them socially or to go out with girls.

Claire never invited me to her parents' home. I never went to Liège which was only ten kilometres away. Some of the farmhands invited me to come with them for a beer or go out with them on the weekends; some meant it genuinely. But I always shrugged off these invitations. I wouldn't expose myself to police checks or raids; it was too dangerous.

After a while the old couple had decided I was working too hard and should have some help. Someone was picked to help me clean out the stables each day.

We became good friends. He was a bachelor who lived in a village nearby and owned a small farm of his own. He was independent—he worked for the widow Roberti to protect himself from deportation to Germany. At the same time he obtained grain and feed for his animals and earned extra money.

This fellow always reported to me what he'd heard on *Radio London*: he listened in the evening when *Radio London* was broadcasting in French to Belgium and told me the latest news each morning—otherwise I wouldn't have known what was going on. I followed the course of the war through him and he also kept me informed on activities and events in the region.

At one point I was thinking of buying a shirt. For several years I'd been wearing the farmer's hand-me-downs and none ever fitted me properly.

My friend said he could buy me a shirt on the black market so I told him to go ahead. He bought a rough shirt of heavy, coarse material with wide green and brown stripes on a white background. I paid four hundred francs for it—a month's wages. I'd worked fourteen to sixteen hours a day for thirty days to earn enough to buy the shirt. Yet, in normal times, I wouldn't have worn such a shirt; I would be ashamed to wear it today.

Once in a while this bachelor invited me to his home: he said we could play cards and visit here and there. Nothing ever came of it, however: there were several villages to pass through on the way to his home and I would have had to come back late at night on my own. Without papers, I didn't want to risk it.

One day the fellow said, "You know, our farmer here is very close to the Germans." A revelation to me, but people in the district were talking about it.

Some time later I was sitting by myself in the stable milking the cows. Suddenly trucks swung into the courtyard. I heard motors spinning, clatter, and German voices.

I tried to crouch between the cows, hoping I wouldn't be seen. But the Germans saw me.

"Get up! Get up! Get up!" was the command. "Where are your papers? Who are you? What are you doing here?"

They were grabbing at me and scouring the place. It was a *razzia*.

I said, "Wait...Look...My papers are upstairs in my room." The officer signalled to a soldier to go with me and check my papers.

The soldier and I went up to my room and I looked around there as if I was searching for papers. Then the German said something I'll never forget.

"*Du bist doch ein armer Teufel.* (You're such a poor devil). Why don't you go to Germany? Your room is so bare. You have nothing here. You're so poor—you don't even have a pair of good pants; you have nothing. In Germany you would be much better off."

I answered, "Sure...but I was born here. I came from here."

He rejoined, "You know, it's..." He was speaking to me half in German, half in French. I showed that I understood German-and he forgot about my papers!

Suddenly the sergeant-major walked in announcing, "O.K.; everything's O.K. Let's go. I checked all the papers downstairs. Everything's in order."

What papers had the farmer shown him? I don't know what happened; I never knew. I never heard any more about it. The old man never mentioned it to me and I never talked to him about it. A strange relationship existed between him and me.

The old man owned a special horse and carriage which he used for visitors. One day he remarked to me, "Jean, you're now in charge of the carriage. You're going to drive it whenever I need you." Sometimes he had guests in the evening after workers had gone home. I was the only one around then.

The first time I drove the carriage he said to me, "Go to the station, Jean, and pick up a German general." He added, "The general knows I'm sending you for him—I told him Jean will pick him up."

So there I was with a comely little horse and carriage. I drove to the station, tied up the horse, and stood at the exit. The general arrived with his adjutant. They saw me and greeted me, "Jean! Jean!"

The general was in high spirits. He and the adjutant shook my hand. They both climbed into the carriage and I drove them to the farm.

I let them out of the carriage and the general gave me a ten-franc tip. Then he and his assistant entered the house.

I heard laughter and toasts over wine from the dining-room that night. There was feasting and drinking and merriment.

They stayed overnight. At six o'clock the next morning, again I was ready with horse and carriage. I took them back to the station and the general gave me another tip.

I repeated this scene many times, for many weeks in a row. The general arrived by train every Wednesday night. I drove him from and to the station. He came for dinner and stayed overnight. He was the military commander of Liège. Obviously my friend the bachelor had spoken the truth: the shrewd old farmer had powerful German connections.

We were well into 1944. From about March of that year I used to see German V-2 rockets streaking across the sky. Often they fell on Liège.

On June the sixth the American and British forces landed in France. Workers on the farm couldn't stop talking about it; they all told me the news.

From then on, my bachelor friend had exciting reports for me daily. He informed me when the Germans were retreating and the underground had begun to be more active; he conveyed the smallest detail to me. He pinpointed the Allied advance. "The Americans and the British are there now. They're coming here; they'll soon be here."

As the Allied armies approached Belgium, local resistance to the Germans began to emerge. One night members of the resistance occupied our farm and captured German soldiers found wandering in the fields—deserters from the German army, mainly Poles or Baltic nationals who'd volunteered or were pressed into military service and were renegades.

My impulse was to join the resistance at the first opportunity: I wanted to be involved in the action. But the guys left swiftly in the middle of the night.

The Germans swept back. They burned down farm after farm trying to smoke out resistance fighters who kept moving around the countryside. The farm next to ours was flattened completely; the Roberti farm wasn't touched. Presumably our boss indeed had the right contacts.

Slowly, gradually, the tenor was changing; the course of the war was changing. One day my co-worker told me the Americans were near at hand, lodging in the area and turning up everywhere in jeeps.

Then an American jeep drove into our courtyard one day. Four Americans were in it. They asked for directions.

I was standing in the courtyard with the widow Roberti. When I saw the Americans enter, I couldn't conceal my joy. The war was coming to an end. An end to a tangle of problems.

I talked to the Americans in English. I lost my self-control; I forgot myself completely.

I hadn't spoken English for about six years; I'd never spoken to an American. But their accents didn't confuse me. I had no difficulty understanding them.

The Americans were surprised when I spoke English. The widow Roberti was speechless.

I showed the Americans around the farm and told them a little about it. A short while later they left.

I remained on the farm doing my job as usual. After my experience with the resistance in Brussels, I wasn't really keen on getting involved with it again; I was more interested in joining a regular army.

The Germans slowly pulled out and left the whole area. The Americans moved in but were still advancing so resistance groups took over and administered everything.

The resistance began to mete out punishment and arrest all types of collaborators. Women who had fraternized with German soldiers were publicly humiliated. And one day thirty or forty resistance fighters carrying guns drove into the farm; their vehicles pulled up in front of the house. They wanted to arrest the old farmer!

Monsieur Degive was standing mute on the front steps. Then suddenly he pointed at me and said, "Ask that man what I've done for him, which side I've really been on, whose side I've been on all along."

The resistance commander turned to me. He walked over and questioned me. "Yeah," I affirmed. "I've been hiding here for almost a year. He protected me; it's only due to him that I'm still alive. What he says is true."

There must have been some speculation and gossip about me locally because the commander and his men believed what I said; they believed the old man and me. The leader ordered his men to withdraw and they left without further question.

The old man never mentioned the incident afterwards; he never talked about it to me even once.

I kept on helping Madame Degive with the bread. She continued to give me a double supper. Everything went on as usual.

A few weeks later, damaged railroad lines were repaired and train travel to Brussels was re-established. I advised Monsieur Degive that I was anxious to visit my uncle in Brussels. The old man knew immediately that I would never come back. His wife knew it, too. They said to me, "Sure. Of course. Goodbye. 'Bye. 'Bye."

I saw in their faces that they knew I would never come back. They knew, too, that I wasn't Jan Van Capelle—that I was somebody else. They had known for some time that I wasn't the person I pretended to be. But they never asked who I was, they never asked me where I'd come from; and I really appreciated that.

The old farmer had saved my life and I'd saved his. We were quits, it would seem; but I owed him much more than he owed me. He was old at the time; I was young, just twenty-two, with my adult life ahead of me.

Admittedly, I'd worked nonstop, every day of the week. I never went out. Workers used to comment, "You work so hard. Why don't you go out on weekends? Have a little fun." Most of them didn't understand what my situation was, but Monsieur Degive understood. And within these narrow limits, he made my life very tolerable. I owe him a great debt for this.

His wife, too, was unusually kind. She was a tough woman; both were tough and stern but, on the scale of virtues, they rated very high.

They liked me so much that they wanted me to stay there permanently. To encourage this they tried to stimulate something between the maid and me: if I would marry Claire, the old lady suggested, they would set us up in a house.

I wasn't eager to adopt any such plans. They wanted me to stay because, as a worker, I wasn't easy to replace; but I needed to return to what, for me, was a more normal life.

I thought maybe I could join the British or American army before the war came to an end. The resistance wasn't doing much militarily and I wanted to hit the Germans where it counted; go after them myself.

CHAPTER XIX
BRUSSELS, 1944

In September 1944 I said good-bye to Fexhe-le-Haut-Clocher and took the train to Brussels. Everything was out in the open there: people were gathering in public places again and Zionists were starting to organize.

In Brussels I felt at liberty for the first time in many years. It was strange to be able to walk around anywhere without running into guards, check posts, or mass arrests.

I went out to Strombeek-Bever to look for Dirk, the painter, and found him there. He told me that after the last time I'd seen him in 1942 he'd hidden a number of Jews. He had been caught, arrested, and sent to a concentration camp. He'd been released and came home not long before my return.

According to Dirk I could get work with the British army; its main supply centre in Europe was located in Brussels. Huge storage depots, especially for food, had been installed in the city. Dirk had worked there briefly and knew that laborers were being hired regularly.

I was taken on at the depot. A satisfying meal was served at noon and the wages were high. With my earnings, I could maintain myself adequately.

Since I was used to hard work, I was able to carry heavy sacks and boxes all day long. We unloaded lorries that arrived from the coast and loaded others that were going to the front. It was a massive undertaking.

While I was moving bags of potatoes I broke my glasses. I had to lift a bag, walk up to a pile, and throw the bag over my head—my glasses soared with the potatoes. The lenses broke.

I had never lost or broken my glasses until then. That afternoon I had the lenses replaced by an optician. The prescription was the same as it had been in 1938 when I left home; my eyes hadn't changed.

One Sunday I decided to ride out to Waterloo and see what was going on there. After an absence of over a year, I dropped in at the farm where I'd worked. The young wife and Fernand were out but his miserly mother was there.

She seemed quite glad to see me. She invited me to sit down and have a cup of coffee. We talked and she told me what had happened in the year I'd been away and brought me up-to-date about people I'd worked with.

Then she asked me to come back to work there! She promised to give me a room. I had just left a much better job than hers and was looking forward to a different kind of life altogether so her offer didn't appeal to me. This time I wasn't in Waterloo to find work; I was just visiting.

My job at the depot held no real challenge for me. I was renting a pleasant room overlooking a beautiful garden—far more agreeable living arrangements than my previous ones had been-and I was able to save some money; but meanwhile I noticed that the American army was advertising for interpreters. I presented myself at the army headquarters, filled out an application, talked to an American officer, and was tested for language proficiency.

I didn't expect anything to materialize from this. One evening, however, when I returned from work, I found a message in my room informing me that someone had called requesting me to be at American headquarters the next morning at ten o'clock, sharp.

I'd already been tested for languages. In German and French I was perfectly fluent. I spoke Dutch and English, too, though my English was less fluent at that time than I would like to think it is today.

At ten o'clock the next morning I appeared as requested. Immediately I was led to an officer who asked, "Are you ready to join us?"

"Yes," I answered. "When?"

"Today," he said.

Jolted, I said, "Oh! Why..?"

He charged ahead. "We don't have much time. There's a war on. We can't wait. Are you willing to attend a swearing-in ceremony this morning?

I'd been waiting for this opportunity; I snatched it. "O.K." I nodded. "Sure."

"Go in right now," he ordered. "We'll swear you in."

The same day, I gave up my room and the few possessions I couldn't carry with me. Several hours later I checked in and was issued a uniform.

I moved out of Brussels with the American army that afternoon.

CHAPTER XX
INTERPRETER IN GERMANY

The first place we came to was Maastricht. Dispatched from Brussels, we arrived in Maastricht—of all places—that evening.

The American army had taken over an old hotel near the railway station. I went to look around; I hadn't been in Maastricht since the middle of 1942.

There was no war damage in Maastricht. I walked to the district where my aunt and her family lived: her house was intact but occupied by strangers. I spoke to some neighbors and none of them could tell me anything about the Schmidts.

I stayed there a few days and used my spare time trying to find people I knew. I'd met many people there in the past.

On the second or third day while roaming around, I saw a familiar face on a balcony. It was Mr. Brunn. He and his wife were staring in my direction; they didn't seem to recognize me. I was in an American uniform.

I called out, "Mr. Brunn, don't you know me? Don't you recognize me?"

"Oh!" he said, "Moishe! It's you!"

"Yeah," I smiled; "it's me. What's happening here, Mr. Brunn? Where's my aunt and the others?"

"Ah," he stammered, "you know...your aunt and the children-your uncle-they all went away; they were taken away. They haven't come back."

The Brunns were Jews from Germany who had lived in Holland a long time. They'd been fairly wealthy. They'd escaped deportation by hiding somewhere; their two daughters had not been in hiding and had been arrested. My relatives, the Schmidts and the two Brunn children were gone.

The Brunns told me about the roundup that took place in the Maastricht area. Jews were herded together and carted away. The elderly Brunns were among the few who were left.

I said to them, "Look, I have to go. We're moving out of Maastricht soon. But whenever I can I'll come and see you."

I did that: whenever I had leave, I went to spend some time with them. Theirs was a hollow existence. Though they hoped at first that their daughters would return, they never did. The old people had lost everything.

I became like a son to them. They looked forward to my visits and pampered me with all kinds of food and fuss.

After I joined the Americans, I found myself facing a sudden counter-offensive by the Germans. In the middle of December the Germans made a fast move across Belgium towards Antwerp. They tried to sever the British from the American troops by splitting through the centre of the Allied front. The action took place a short distance from our position.

During three days of dense fog, German paratroopers dropped from the skies. American soldiers didn't know who was who: they were calling to one another, thinking the Germans were standing right beside them.

I was south of Maastricht at the time. My unit didn't know all the details but we knew there was fighting very close to us.

Then the sun came out. The German push was cut off; the Battle of the Bulge was over. This was the only engagement in which my company was imperilled.

After that we moved into Germany. I had never dreamed of ending up there. It was just by a stroke of luck in signing on as an interpreter that suddenly I was returning to Germany.

I experienced a strange feeling when I crossed the border in an American uniform. The crossing point was southeast of Maastricht and fierce fighting was going on there. Planes and bombs were screaming around us.

For the first time I saw German cities completely destroyed. The cities we drove through were endless rubble; there was almost nothing left. Walls had tumbled down. We had to be careful where we stepped.

Generally, my group moved into an area immediately after it had been bombed. We were sometimes the first ground force to push forward.

There were several soldiers with me once when we were ordered to occupy a specific building. The Germans were still shooting from the rooftops at the time, yet I felt fearless and I recall running way ahead of the other guys.

Astounded they asked, "How come you're running ahead of us? What do you think you're doing? Aren't you scared?

I answered exultantly, "No! I'm not scared. I'm happy!" And I forged ahead even faster. They couldn't understand it.

Afterwards they insisted on talking about my behavior. Some of the guys were perceptive and intelligent; a few were college graduates. They questioned me, "How come you're not scared?"

"Because I know you guys are scared," I answered. Several had suffered emotional collapse.

"I am enjoying this war," I told them. "I've been longing for combat for years. I only wish I could fight more! I haven't fought enough!"

I'd been suppressed for years. The Nazis had muzzled me; they had almost crushed me. I hadn't been able to make a move. Thinking of what they'd done to me made me ache to tear them apart.

I wanted to fight, to take revenge. I had to vent my rage.

We moved northwards in Germany. We were on the west side of the Rhine and the German army withdrew over the river to the east side.

I was stationed then in Krefeld, less than one hundred kilometres from Wattenscheid, but Wattenscheid was still in German hands. The Rhine divided the two sides and artillery firing from both banks was ferocious.

My unit was billeted in a rich man's villa outside Krefeld. In it we discovered a large wine cellar full of bottles of choice German wine.

This sparked the longest party of my life. We all shared the spoils. I drank six bottles of wine, four litres or a gallon, by myself; I drank bottle after bottle without stopping.

I remember being deliriously happy! I sang and played the fool—the happiest man in the world and utterly drunk. Eventually I couldn't move without falling down.

We emptied the whole cellar to the last bottle. I was out of commission for at least three days; I couldn't get up. I was in a sodden haze.

None of our group reported for duty. We couldn't; we were wrecked for three days. Officers, men—everyone.

We were never reprimanded for this and the incident stays in my mind as a celebration of the Nazi defeat. A Hallelujah Victory Celebration. I had a wonderful time.

We were still on the west side of the Rhine; the east side was held by the Germans. Their batteries kept blasting across the river, destroying their own cities in order to hit us.

I was never involved in the battles that were going on; I was kept behind the front line. Sometimes, however, I had to go forward to investigate or interrogate.

The army was taking German prisoners and some were high-ranking officers. We needed to pry information from them about German positions and the strength of their troops.

The questioning was conducted fairly, unlike what I'd experienced with the Gestapo. The captives were seated in a room and we talked to them; the technique wasn't harsh. I never saw any brutality.

Sometimes we captured an SS man trying to pass himself off as an ordinary soldier. Though I was supposed to be only the translator, in cases like these I participated in the questioning by bringing out points the Americans had not thought of. I was well aware of SS crimes.

The 'Black Shirts,' however, never gave a straight answer; they feigned innocence and denied everything. It was difficult to deal with them: I felt like taking a stick and beating them over the head—of applying their own methods to themselves. The Americans wouldn't tolerate such tactics so, in some ways, I felt under restraint. I had to sit and listen to the garbage they spewed out.

Interrogations of regular officers were much simpler; the Americans tried to deal with these on a soldier to soldier basis. Strategy and emplacements and military strength were what mainly interested them, as well as the civilian situation on the other side of the Rhine. The American army had to plan its advance into Germany so as to minimize the loss in human lives. The war was still being fought and, at that time, the Americans weren't much interested in probing into criminal responsibility.

The Americans made a distinction between the regular army and the SS, knowing that soldiers would ultimately be released whereas the SS might be brought to trial; they therefore guarded the SS more securely. During interrogations, however, the distinction never came out because, as yet, we had no witnesses or evidence against the individual SS officer. Suspecting that a particular person had been a concentration camp guard wasn't proof and we didn't have the mandate to pursue such suspicions. It was often exasperating.

Even after they had lost the west side of the Rhine, the Germans still believed they would win in the end. The prisoners we took were very defiant; they weren't ready to give in. Their defiance annoyed me more than anything else. When it was obvious to the rest of the world that they were whipped, they still acted like the master race.

Often we captured soldiers of fifteen or sixteen. They knew next to nothing but were fanatic Nazis: I was shocked by the fanaticism still rampant in Germany. I was horrified to find that belief in Hitler was stronger in 1945 than it had been when I left seven years earlier. It was alarming. The Germans believed their government's propaganda that they had really won the war, but had been betrayed by a mysterious force. They couldn't grasp that Hitler had lost the war; this was an impossibility to them.

While I was stationed in Krefeld, I met a German who identified himself to me as a Jew. He told me he'd been living in Krefeld with a German family. I don't know if it was true or not; he may have been a Nazi who chose hastily to call himself a Jew—a safe cover suddenly whereas, previously, it had been the greatest offense in history. Allied victories made an enormous difference for Europeans on the allied side of the front line in this respect so I was disinclined to believe the man's story.

From Krefeld I moved south along the Rhine to Koblenz, then up the Rhine to Mainz. When we could finally cross the Rhine River, in March or April 1945, I was posted in Würzburg.

The allied armies moved in different directions across Germany: one moved south, another north, one east, and one west; I was attached to the army in the south. My unit never came across any concentration camps.

Then we began to hear the horror stories. When the camps were liberated by allied troops, photographs of the survivors and ghastly reports appeared in the world press. What went on in the camps became common knowledge. And none of it surprised me. I was shocked only by the extremes to which the Nazis had gone. I'd known that many people would die under their heel—I hadn't imagined the numbers would be so great.

At the end of April 1945 we heard that Hitler had killed himself. We weren't sure if it was true—there were rumors it wasn't. He had said he would fight from the mountains of Bavaria; we were close to that area and expected to have to keep on fighting. It was a time full of rumors and uncertainties though we were confident that the war would end soon.

We read the army newspaper, *The Stars and Stripes,* eagerly every day. One day it was headlined: WAR ENDS.

May 7, 1945, the Germans signed the surrender simultaneously in Reims, France, and Berlin. War in Europe was over.

We all congratulated each other and expressed deep satisfaction. The end of the war against so threatening and powerful an enemy was indeed a great occasion.

The American soldiers were happy that they'd be able to return home. There were parties and festivities among us. It was a grand holiday.

I stayed on in the army of occupation. The American sector was mainly in the south. The part of Germany where I came from was under British command. The French occupied the sector near Strasbourg and the Russians were in what was then East Germany.

With the war over, my unit became involved in civilian administration. I was an interpreter in many cases investigating irregularities, crimes, or disputes.

The languages I used were German, English, and occasionally French. The first time I encountered some French Canadian soldiers I guessed they were talking French but scarcely understood what they were saying. It sounded strange to me. When they switched, more or less, to European French, we communicated with each other more readily.

Each of the allied armies had an engineering division that was rebuilding the sector's railroads. My unit was assigned to the railroad system to help keep American supplies and personnel moving through the country. I worked around train stations then.

A few times I thought of visiting Wattenscheid. The distance was under 350 kilometres (little more than 200 miles) but transit lines were still disrupted. There was widespread wreckage and the trains weren't running on schedule.

Also, Wattenscheid was in the British zone. It wasn't easy to travel between zones-we needed special permission—and I didn't expect to find anyone there whom I particularly cared to see so I didn't pursue it.

My plan was to go back to Holland eventually. I'd been admitted there before the war with a valid visa; I could resume my interrupted journey from there to Israel.

Holland was liberated at the very end of the war, a few days before the surrender. Formidable combat continued there much longer than in other areas with Canadian troops fighting alongside the British.

I couldn't travel to Amsterdam or Franeker until the war was over and then it took months to repair the railroads. I followed the progress through reports in newspapers.

The longer I stayed with the army the more I felt it was a waste of time. There was nothing I could learn. It wasn't interesting. It was peacetime service, working a routine shift and eating huge meals.

The food was ample, of every variety and no stinting of it: we could eat as much as we wanted. It was all brought from the United States in cans and packages. The quality and quantity were much greater than had been available during the war.

On my first morning in the army in Maastricht, I ate twelve eggs for breakfast. I hadn't eaten eggs for years: the farmers hadn't kept hens because they required too much feed. I got very sick as a result of my greed.

Even afterwards when I ate less greedily, I suffered diarrhoea for several weeks before adjusting to the rich diet. Then, where food was concerned, the army was ideal. Mess had become its best feature.

I also learned fluent English-American army English, of course. The soldiers came from many parts of the United States and told me all kinds of things about the country and life there. They talked of black citizens. There were no blacks in my outfit; they were segregated from whites and served in different units. Many were truck drivers.

I met a few Jews from New York and New Jersey. I met many people; but, despite this, it did not seem particularly interesting at the time.

Actually, I hated being in Germany. I was full of resentment toward the nation.

My work was directly with trains, railroad workers and passengers. Sometimes survivors of concentration camps came through on trains and I talked to them. They told me horrible stories about the camps.

Once in a while I was given leave. I had free passes to travel on trains so I managed to visit the Brunns a few times.

I had to travel from Würzburg to Maastricht via Liège where I changed trains. I had lived near Liège for a year but had never been there. When I finally got there, I could see it was large and sprawling and, no doubt, a fine city. Nevertheless, the only part I walked through was the station; I felt no attachment to the place.

On a visit to the Brunns one evening in mid-1945 I arrived in Maastricht late because the train had been delayed. At the door of the house I met a girl; she was searching for a key. I didn't know who she was. Finally she found the key and unlocked the door.

She knew about me from the Brunns and let me into the house; we went in together. The Brunns were out.

I asked her who she was and heard her story. She was living with the Brunns, who were trying to adopt her. She was a German-Jewish girl whose parents had been killed by the Nazis. She'd been hidden for several years by some miners in the district of Maastricht. She was eighteen years of age and engaged to marry a Jewish man who owned a small shop in Heerlen, an industrial town near Maastricht.

The Brunns returned home and we all sat down to a meal. I'd brought food packets in my bag.

I stayed at the Brunns for a number of days and sometimes talked to Shoshana. She wasn't around very often.

I was paid regularly by the army and was issued two hundred cigarettes every week. I wasn't a smoker so I sold the cigarettes. Altogether, at long last, I was accumulating a sizable sum of money.

There was nowhere to spend money. Würzburg, for instance, was a city in ruins. Few buildings were standing. My unit was living in railroad cars.

So I saved all my money. I couldn't deposit it anywhere—it had to be on me; that was the safest place. I kept it in my pocket or under my pillow as before. Then, when I visited the Brunns, I left my savings with them.

When I was able to travel to Brussels, I decided to spend a leave visiting my friend Dirk. I stuffed my duffel bag with food and cigarettes, soap and razor blades-all kinds of scarce items; I wanted to repay his many kindnesses and his friendship toward me.

I went out to Strombeek-Bever and found him at home. His wife was there, too. They'd just become proud parents.

Dirk was so happy to see me. He welcomed me with warmth. I unpacked all the goodies I'd brought, and he and his wife danced with delight. I spent a few glowing days with them.

I visited the Brunns several times during that year, 1945. Each time I met Shoshana. She would ask me about the army and about Germany: she hadn't been out of a narrow neck of Holland for many years and she was curious about other places.

The Germans slowly took over the railroad system; the Americans had handed it back to them. We remained in charge of the railroad workers and were still checking the trains, but I felt that I was frittering away my time. There wasn't much to do.

One day a Jewish girl came to our office at the station. She was on her way from Frankfurt to Munich and complained that she couldn't find a seat on the train.

I said, "I'll try to get you a seat." I went with her into a first-class carriage. A German was sitting there, an arrogant man who looked like an SS type. I could imagine him flicking a whip and lashing out at people. I couldn't bear the sight of the man.

I said to him, "Is this your seat?" I spoke to him in German. He didn't answer me. He pretended he didn't hear me; he didn't see me.

I repeated, "Is this your seat?" No response.

I grabbed him by the coat. I demanded, "Is this your seat?"

He answered, "Yes. Yes." Each word was like gunshot.

"Where's your ticket?" I persisted.

He showed me his ticket. I snapped, "Get up! Get up!" and I told the girl, "This is your seat now. You sit here."

I don't know if his ticket was for that seat; I didn't look at it. All I saw was a *fahrbissener* (rabid, fanatical) Nazi. I said to him, "Come with me."

He sat motionless. He didn't budge.

I pulled him up. I shoved him.

He was bigger than me, tall and solid, a heavy-weight; I was no more than middleweight. But I had an American uniform on and I was seething with anger.

I pushed him forward. I drove him along the platform. He barely moved so I shoved him like they used to shove me. I hit him in the ribs like they hit me, like they hit so many of us.

I ordered, "Go on. Faster. Move! Move! Faster! Faster!" I grew angrier by the minute, more and more excited.

He reached the top of the staircase leading down from the platform. Again he didn't move. I shoved him. Then I kicked him. I kicked him so hard that he rolled right down the stairs.

He lay at the bottom and didn't get up. I walked away. I left him there. I paid no more attention to him.

Some Americans working in the station saw what happened and objected to my actions. "You're not supposed to do that," they said. "We're going to report you."

"I had to do that," I countered. "It's my job. The guy's a Nazi—he behaves and looks like a Nazi. I had to do that. You do what you want. If you want to report me, report me."

They reported me to a senior officer. They said that while I was on duty I had hit a German passenger and thrown him down the stairs.

A major was in command of our unit. I was summoned to his office. "What happened?" he demanded. "What were you doing?"

I replied, "Major, that was my revenge." He knew something about my experiences. He knew I'd been in the underground army.

"I had to do that," I explained. "I had to get it out of my system. Penalize me if you want to; do what you want."

"Forget it," he grumbled. "I haven't seen anything; I don't know anything. Only don't do it again."

Later the other soldiers told me they had taken the German to the hospital. His arms and three ribs were broken.

I had really let go. I had to deal with Germans every day and I couldn't pay them back for what they'd done to me and others.

I never mixed with Germans. I kept to the American compound; I could live there in complete isolation. The army had its own supplies, its own canteen, American movies and entertainment.

The major commanding our unit wanted to recommend me for officers' training school and the regular army. He laid out the opportunities for me: "You can go to the United States. You can get an immigration visa, become an American citizen."

I enjoyed my association with the Americans—I found them refreshing compared to Europeans. But I wasn't interested in their enticements at the time. My plan was to go to Israel; I had no other goal. After all that I'd been through, I was convinced that there wasn't a future for Jews anywhere but in Israel.

It seemed to me that even Americans didn't like Jews very much. I noticed that some American Jews were always looking over their shoulders to see if they'd said the right thing and done the right thing.

After a while the army days grew longer and longer. I decided the time had come to resume my fitful journey to Israel. I resigned from the army.

CHAPTER XXI
RETURN TO HOLLAND

Early in January, 1946 I went to the Brunns' in Maastricht. I was back in civvies again.

I asked Mr. Brunn for my money and he told me that a few weeks earlier, the Dutch Secret Police had searched the house hunting for black-market goods and money; they'd rummaged everywhere. They'd missed finding my money by a hair's-breadth. It was stashed among the linens.

I left Maastricht and took a train up north. The trains were running again, but travel was slow and often interrupted; many bridges hadn't been rebuilt.

I spent about two days getting to Franeker. I arrived and found that everything there looked the same. Nothing had changed.

I took a room in a small hotel. The next morning I went to the town hall.

In most West European countries, every resident is registered in the local city hall. This was the custom in Holland.

I presented myself to the town clerk. "My name is Moritz Schnitzer. I lived here in Franeker for a few years until late 1941; I was registered in this office. I'm a Jew from Germany; I'm stateless; the Nazis took away my citizenship—you've heard what happened."

"I've lost all my papers because of the war. You know what happened during the war—we were all pushed from place to place. I lost my resident visa and my Dutch work permit; now I need to establish my identity."

He stared at me. "What? What's this you're saying? Is it true what you said?"

"Sure it's true!" I answered. "Ask some other people." He was a young man. "Ask older people—they'll tell you it's true."

Dumbfounded, he answered, "All right. What's your name? I'll look it up in my files."

He scanned some files and returned about five minutes later holding a paper. "Moritz Schnitzer. Yes. You died in 1942."

"What do you mean?" I exclaimed. "How could I have died in 1942? Don't you see me here? I'm here. It's 1946. I'm standing in front of you—I'm not dead."

"It says you're dead. And it has the official stamp."

"I don't care if it's stamped or not," I protested. "I'm here right in front of you. How can I be dead?" I pointed at the document. "See the picture? It looks like me doesn't it?"

"Yeah," he agreed. "It looks like you."

"Then how can I be dead if I'm standing in front of you?"

He was stumped. "I don't know what we can do. I can't do anything about it. You're dead and that's that."

The death had been certified by someone in the local administration. The Germans had probably furnished a list naming people who were dead and no one had questioned it.

I said, "Look, there has been a mistake. There has to be a solution."

He finally conceded. "I'll talk to the mayor."

The mayor was in his office. The clerk went up to consult him.

Soon the mayor came down and questioned me. "You're one of the Jewish boys who was here before?"

"Yes, I am," I asserted.

"I see. That's very interesting," he said. Still hesitating he repeated, "Is this true what you're saying?"

"Certainly it's true," I replied. "You see my picture there. I know this place. I've been here before. I'm no stranger to Franenker. I lived here for two years."

He relented. "Sit down for a few minutes." He searched through a law book and a code of regulations, then he said, "All right. If you can bring me a witness who'll testify that you are Moritz Schnitzer, then we'll fill out all the papers for you and give you an identification card."

My one recourse was to go to a farmer I'd worked for. Maybe the farmer would recognize me and be my witness.

I walked out of the building and along the main street. I passed the old train station; the structure was still there.

I continued down the Harlingerweg toward the farm that used to be situated three minutes by bicycle from the *hachshara.* There I turned in.

A farm laborer saw me. He recognized me right away! He gasped, "Ah, Mose!" They had called me 'Mose' on that farm.

He came over and embraced me! Then he called the farmer.

The farmer came out; his name was Van der Berg. "Mose!" he cried. "You!" And he kissed me!

There were tears in his eyes—A Friesian farmer crying! I had always thought those people had no emotions. My unexpected return had fractured a deep reserve.

The next thing the farmer did was take me into his living-room. I had never seen the living-room before; I had always been in the stable.

Then he sat me down in the kitchen. He said, "You must eat with us."

I saw his two sons—they knew me, too; they had worked with me. And his wife remembered me. What a *simcha* (celebration) it was! An unbelievable reception.

Van der Berg kept saying, "I'm so happy to see you and that you're alive! I'm so happy! We talked about you all the time. We wondered what had happened to all the boys and girls...what had happened to all of you. It has been so long... so many years; no news. People said that all of you died and now you're here."

These people were religious believers. To them, it was as if I'd come back from the dead. They were awed to see me alive.

The farmer himself offered to accompany me to the town hall. He said immediately, "I'll take my bike. You take my son's bike." And away we went.

We entered the town hall and the office of the mayor. Van der Berg declared, "Of course Mose is Mose! I know him! Sure! It's true what he says!" And he signed papers, affidavits, as my witness.

That cleared the detritus from my life. I could be my own self again. in Franeker in 1941 I'd lost my true identity when I fled the Gestapo sweep; in the same place about five years later I regained it.

It's difficult to explain the effects of living with a false identity. When I changed my name to Jan Van Capelle, I knew that I had to conceal many aspects of my personality. In a sense, I had to cease being the type of person I'd been until then. To achieve this I censored everything I said and did; I controlled myself every minute. I mumbled or said nothing so as not to reveal too much. This was very hard to do sometimes: people tend to equate silence with unfriendliness and resent it.

With false identities, I no longer felt German. I felt like nothing I had ever been. I had had to earn my daily bread by the sweat of my brow at the lowest level of society. Like an actor, I had had to play a role—to appear to be dull and crude without education or refinement. Reading or discussions had been banned.

Both as Jan Van Capelle and Eli Hart, I couldn't disclose that I had any special knowledge of Germany or personal relationship to Germany. Otherwise, as Eli Hart I was able to reveal more nearly who I was.

The problem with false identities was that I was generally with other people; I slept and worked beside other people. And I couldn't afford to give myself away by chattering asleep or awake. I was concerned that, when I was sleeping, someone might get information from me that I wouldn't want to divulge. I was always afraid that someone might question me some day or something might happen to unmask me. But it never happened. No one had ever said anything to me about something I didn't want known or hadn't deliberately told.

However, I'd had enough of being someone else. I was tired of withholding so much and expecting to be discovered. I wanted my own identity again.

Now I had it. I had received an identification card.

I thanked van der Berg and said good-bye to him. I was leaving Franeker and going to Amsterdam.

CHAPTER XXII
AMSTERDAM, 1945

I had to wait around for the one train a day. The Germans had seized many railway cars and taken them to Germany. Few passenger cars were available at that time; we travelled under primitive conditions in freight cars. At last, a couple of days later, I reached Amsterdam—*Makom* (The Place) as the Friesians called the city.

I thought it would now be simple to obtain ration tickets, which were still in use; basic foods were rationed. Also, I needed an updated visa to stay in Holland.

I went to the city hall in Amsterdam and learned that, before being issued these papers, I would have to see the Secret Police. "Many war criminals are sneaking in here. We can't give out anything before you get clearance."

I hurried to the Secret Police. Three or four people were ahead of me. They were under great strain.

My turn arrived. I told the policeman who I was and that I'd been on *hachshara* in Holland until the end of 1941. I added a few more facts.

The policeman observed, "You are *Yehud*i" (a Jew).

I replied, "Yes, of course. You know what we went through, all of us."

He nodded. "Sure," and gave me the necessary clearance. "You're kosher now," he remarked. He happened to be a Jew!

I walked out with my clearance papers and returned to the city hall. I'd had a visa before the war; now it was renewed. I was a legal resident of Holland again.

By January 1946, the Mizrachi Organization was running a residence in Amsterdam for people who were planning to settle in Israel. Men who'd been in the Jewish Brigade of the British Army had founded this residence which was called a *Beth Chalutz* (pioneer house). It had sleeping and eating accommodations for displaced people so I stayed there on my return to Amsterdam.

Meanwhile the Zionist group I'd been affiliated with was about to set up a new *hachshara* in Dieren-Doesberg near Arnhem. It had been started from scratch about two weeks after I arrived in Amsterdam because people like me were surfacing after all the years.

The only other person to reappear from the group that had been located in Franeker was Bram, the Dutch fellow who'd escaped with me in November 1941. After he and I had split up, he'd succeeded in crossing over to England. There he'd joined the Dutch army-in-exile.

Things balance out in strange ways. In 1941 I had probably saved Bram's life. Then after the war, he was the source of a momentous turn in my life.

I met him in Amsterdam in January 1946. Through him, my brother subsequently learned that I was alive: Bram mentioned me to a friend in England who knew my brother and that person told Eddi about me.

I was in residence in Amsterdam when I received a telegram from Eddi. It came from Canada and read:

OVERJOYED TO HEAR YOU ARE ALIVE. I AM O.K. CABLE ANSWER ABOUT EVERYTHING. WILL SEND PARCELS, MONEY. WIFE AND I WILL SEE YOU HERE SOON.
LOVE,
EDMUND

I cabled an answer immediately to let him know I'd received the telegram. He wrote me by airmail the same day outlining details of his past five years and formulating plans. His cable and letter were dated February 5, 1946, one day after my twenty-fourth birthday.

CHAPTER XXIII
ON HACHSHARA IN DIEREN-DOESBERG

I moved to the hachshara at Dieren-Doesberg a few days later; I wrote to Eddi from there. I wasn't thinking seriously about his proposal to go to Canada; I was set on going to Israel.

I was the only survivor of Franeker to participate in the new *hachshara*. Bram didn't rejoin because he'd contracted tuberculosis during the war. Since I had been on hachshara before, the organizers put me in charge. I was the most experienced person there.

In Dieren I did something that Rabbi Yehoshua Wolf had wanted me to do earlier: I gave the religious lessons. I performed all the functions that Rabbi Wolf had performed in Franeker.

We built a busy *hachshara*. We had between twenty-five and thirty members, most of us working on farms as we'd done in Franeker. This time, however, we sent some members to learn trades.

I myself went back to farming—by now it was easy for me. I enjoyed it, too; I found the work satisfying compared to working in an army of occupation.

Some of us worked on contract as was common in Belgium during the sugar-beet season. Teams of us took on specialized jobs for farmers. We worked very hard.

We also enrolled in a study program at a local agricultural school. In response to our request for instruction in theoretical farming, the principal gave us an initial course on the chemistry of soils and fertilizers; I picked it up very fast. This surprised me since I hadn't studied much chemistry before. At the Adath Israel Gymnasium in Berlin I'd done a little science but forgotten all of it. And this was eight years later.

I memorized every formula our instructor wrote down,

quickly and accurately. He said to me one day, "In all the years that I've been teaching, I've never had a student who grasped a subject as fast as you do."

I took several more of his courses and he got to know me well. Then he said to me, "I'd like to send you to the Agricultural University in Wageningen. I want to sponsor you."

He was mentally stimulated by teaching our eager group and appreciated my learning ability. Usually he taught slow-witted or uninterested farm boys and couldn't drive anything into their heads. To my astonishment—and provoking some thought—he was offering me a college education at his own expense.

Our courses were given in the evenings because of our daytime work. I was attending a class when someone came to fetch me. "There's a phone call for you from Canada."

We didn't have a phone in the *hachshara* so I went to take the call in a hotel. Eddi was on the line with his father-in-law. "We're glad you survived the war, Moishe," his father-in-law said. "Now we want you to come to Canada."

I told him, "Thanks for the invitation but I want to go to Israel. I've been preparing myself to go for seven years since 1939. That's why I'm here on *hachshara*... "

I had started the hachshara; I was in charge of it. I couldn't leave the group. I explained this to Eddi and his father-in-law.

Afterwards, just as they had at the start of the war, the British blockaded Israel. Legal immigration was impossible. The only way to enter was covertly on what was called 'Aliyah Beth.' This method was a roundabout and dangerous process; some Jews who tried it lost their lives in the attempt. Most who came from camps for displaced persons in Europe were turned back and interned by the British in Cyprus and elsewhere; they were often detained for months.

I continued writing to my brother while still planning to go to Israel. I was helping build an active organization in Holland. We now had several hundred members.

Then who arrived in Dieren? Unexpectedly, Shoshana. She suddenly appeared and wanted to join the kibbutz.

"I thought you were going to marry a man from Heerlen; I thought you were engaged to him!" She had always given me the impression that she would be married soon.

"I was engaged to marry him, yes, but I couldn't go through with it. I didn't like him that much."

She became a member of the *hachshara* in Dieren; she left Maastricht and moved in with us. We saw more and more of each other; I fell in love with her. And she with me.

I'd impressed her as experienced; I'd knocked around. The other man was settled in Heerlen—a not too exciting life.

Shoshana was a talented artist, a potter. She was attractive with black hair and big brown eyes; and after a while I asked her to marry me.

She was under twenty-one and a ward of the state: after the war, the Dutch authorities had begun to take an interest in orphaned Jewish children because of pressure from the churches. The Protestant Church, for example, had been trying to convert some children who'd been saved by church members during the war. The state therefore assumed guardianship of these children.

To marry Shoshana, I needed permission from the state. So I went to to the Ministry of Social Welfare in Amsterdam and explained my situation to the officials.

They made all kinds of complications. They said that I had no income and wasn't settled. As the ones responsible for deciding what was in her best interests, they refused permission for the marriage.

I told Shoshana, "We can't get married here but we'll be leaving Holland; the government will have no jurisdiction over you then. We'll get married in France on our way to Israel. It isn't much of a problem."

Everyone in the kibbutz knew our plans; we spent all our spare time together. Whenever I was called to Amsterdam, apparently she was painfully lonely.

On occasion I had to be in Amsterdam at our head office. I'd become secretary of Bachad, the Young Mizrachi of Holland; I was the senior member of the organization for a time.

We had a group of fifty or sixty members in Amsterdam. I devoted considerable energy to organizing the group.

In Amsterdam I always stayed in a hostel called the Joodse Invalide. Jewish people of all ages lived there. It was the only public place in the city where one could eat kosher food.

I met my distant cousin, Avram Heller there. He was the younger brother of Moishe Heller who'd been with me on *hachshara* in Franeker.

Avram's father and mother had survived the war and were staying at the hostel. Avram had come from his kibbutz in Israel to be with them; at the same time, he was acting as *shaliach* (envoy) for the Kibbutz Hadati movement, a branch of the Bachad. He spent about a year in Holland.

Avram and I worked side by side in the Mizrachi Organization. Since I was familiar with Dutch conditions and he was a first-rate organizer, he advised me on what should be done and helped me to carry out programs.

I met hardly any Jews I'd known before. I tried to find the Kosters in Amsterdam and was told that, a few months after I'd left his home, Professor Koster had been arrested—on the grounds that he wasn't wearing a yellow star. The only one of his family to survive the war was the deranged child, who'd been placed in a non-Jewish home.

I tried to locate members of my family when I reached Amsterdam in 1946. I haunted the refugee agencies and checked every register. Jewish groups including the Zionist Organization, plus the Red Cross and United Nations, had established offices in West European countries and were actively tracing and resettling people: they published lists of survivors and tried to locate relatives; it was a massive international effort. But my parents' names and Benno's never emerged.

I continued my search for many years. I pursue this information to this day.

Eddi, too, made inquiries through Canadian, American, and English organizations. We tried to locate anyone we'd known who was missing.

When reports described how the Nazis had killed six million Jews, I was still optimistic that Benno, at least, had survived: he had youth and strength to his advantage. But slowly I accepted the fact that Eddi and I were probably the only ones alive in our immediate family. My parents, my brother Benno, my paternal grandmother, the Schmidts, the Brunn girls, the group in Franeker, Piefke Levy, and many others had disappeared.

Passover 1946 arrived. We were scheduled to leave Holland after the holiday; the entire group on *hachshara* was planning to move down to Marseille to board a boat for Israel.

I spent Passover in Maastricht with the Brunns. Shoshana was there, too.

The holiday was interrupted by a call from our head office asking me to come to Amsterdam immediately. I hurried there and found our leaders assembled, Avram Heller among them. They enjoined on me to wait in Holland and not rush to Marseille: I would get stuck in Marseille, they warned, and wouldn't be able to stir from there for some time. I would be more useful to the movement by remaining in Holland.

I returned to Maastricht and reported this to Shoshana. She exploded with anger: she accused me of delaying and betraying her, of renouncing the marriage. She stormed that my refusal to go to France after Passover was because I didn't want to marry her.

I tried to explain that I had no authority to go to Marseille—none of our group could go; she wasn't free to go either. But she misconstrued the situation, and railed that it was all my doing—that I'd manipulated the council into postponing our departure. Then she broke off our engagement.

She was blaming me when, in fact, political events had militated against our going. What hurt me most was her urging me to go with her to France, as previously planned, despite the council's decision. She refused to understand that it would have been rash to do it.

We both stayed at the *hachshara*. That summer I became more involved with running the head office and organizing the Amsterdam group so I took a room at the *Joodse Invalide* for a few months.

The year was drifting by. A symphony orchestra was formed in Arnhem and concerts began. Some members of the *hachshara* were musically trained so, in the fall of 1946, the group decided to attend a series of concerts. There was a concert every month and I became quite fond of classical music.

The Concertgebouw Orchestra had given concerts when I lived in Amsterdam in 1941-1942. The Kosters attended those concerts; I never did because I kept away from public gatherings. After the war, however, I heard the Concertgebouw Orchestra in its concert hall in Amsterdam.

Whenever I went to Dieren, I saw Shoshana. I still cared for her very much and she seemed to feel something for me, too, but we kept our distance.

Our organization continued to hold us back, stalling everything. The leaders declared that a chance to leave would come before long. "Don't move," they said. "The border to Israel will open one day soon. Stay put for now."

My brother was writing to me regularly, repeating, "Come to Canada. You can study here; you were always a good student. If you come, you'll be able to develop yourself, do what you want to do. If you go to a kibbutz in Israel, you'll never be able to study."

By then, in my twenty-fifth year, I knew that if I didn't study soon, I would never study. I'd never yet seen the outside of a university, let alone the inside. And I'd always dreamed of studying something, of being somebody someday. Here I was. After twenty-five years my greatest achievement was surviving the war. I had no other achievement.

Eddi dangled the bait before me continually. He asserted, "You have an obligation to educate yourself. You haven't done so yet; you didn't have the opportunity. Come to Canada. You'll have the opportunity."

After a while I began to think, "Here I am, sitting in Holland. I can't go to Israel. I'm bogged down in nowhere land. I have wasted time in jails, then with the army. Now I'm in the same fix again."

Our leaders counselled, "Be patient. Run the *hachshara* until we're ready to move." They hesitated to risk having too many people interned by the British. It was a very trying period.

Early in 1947 I discussed the situation with Avram Heller. I put all the facts to him and asked him, "What should I do?" He knew my history; I'd told him everything. Now I underlined the point "I have a chance to study."

Avram agreed with Eddi's opinion. "If you go to Israel, you'll end up in a kibbutz. You'll have no chance to study. Now you have a chance to study; go!"

He himself had lived in a kibbutz in Israel since about 1936. "If you have a chance to study," he said, "study. Then come to Israel after you've finished."

This was the compromise he proposed. This was the solution.

I was leaning in that direction of my own accord. I'd been coming to the conclusion that my life had been miserable enough. As I had a chance to educate myself, I thought I should do so. And Avram helped me to reach that decision.

When I announced my plan, Shoshana heard about it and confronted me again. She told me not to go to Canada. She was afraid that, if I went, she would never see me again. She wanted me to go to Israel as she still was planning to do. She suggested we should marry, as we planned before.

By now I was wary of her. I'd often seen her moody and sensed it would be difficult for me to deal with her. She tended to put pressure on me impulsively.

We became quite close again. She urged me not to go, to stay with her. However, I was determined to go.

I realized I couldn't take Shoshana with me. My brother was living with his in-laws. He could only accommodate one person; he couldn't look after a couple—it would be too heavy a burden on him.

So I told Shoshana that, later on, if we still felt strongly about each other and if it was materially possible, I would try to bring her to Canada. This didn't satisfy or convince her.

CHAPTER XXIV
ON THE WAY TO CANADA

Eddi then obtained a visa for me. Near the end of January 1947, he wrote to tell me the visa was on its way by surface mail and would reach The Hague in two months' time. I was then to present myself to the Canadian Embassy in The Hague.

I needed an additional travel document. I had only the identification card I'd obtained in Franeker. So I went to the Dutch police and requested a document that would permit me to travel. They refused to give it to me. "You're not Dutch," they explained.

"Then how can I travel?" I demanded. "I'm stateless. But I have a chance to go to Canada—and you can get rid of me."

Whenever I'd applied for an extension of my visa, I'd been given the run-around: the police had conveyed clearly that I wasn't welcome. Now I flung at them, "I'm not welcome here, so why don't you give me a chance to leave? Give me a travel document and I'll leave; you'll be rid of me. you won't have to deal with me any more."

They wouldn't do it. They refused to do anything.

In March I finally went to the Foreign Office in The Hague. I told the officials there, "I'd like to get a document so I can leave the country. I don't want to stay here any longer; I'm disgusted with this country."

I was blunt and brutally frank. "You don't want me. I don't want you. So give me a travel document. Then I can go."

About a week later they sent me a document. It was an identity certificate for use by aliens travelling from Holland to other countries.

In April I presented myself at the Canadian embassy. The prospective immigrants there were all women, war brides who wanted to join their husbands in Canada; I was the only man.

Very few displaced people were immigrating as yet—it was too soon after the war. In fact, as odd as it sounds, Canada still had no Minister of Immigration: the Immigration Branch was part of the Department of Mines and Resources!

I spoke to the Visa Officer who told me that I needed to have a medical check-up. After the check-up, I went back to him and, examining the chart, he said, "Everything is O.K."

He was about to stamp the visa in my travel document when he recalled, "You have to buy a ticket before I can give you the visa. You need a boat or airplane ticket for Canada; then come back for the visa."

I hied myself to the KLM office and did I have *tsuris* (trouble) there! No one would sell me a ticket. "How come you won't sell me a ticket?" I asked. "I have a visa waiting for me."

I told Royal Dutch Airline officials, too, that I wanted to get out of Holland. They could get rid of me. That tactic often worked for some reason: they sold me a ticket which I paid for with the money I'd saved while I was with the American army. The ticket was very expensive: it cost about one thousand dollars for a one-way fare from Amsterdam to Montreal.

The Canadian official then stamped the immigrant visa into my travel document. I was ready to go.

Before going on to Canada, I intended to visit relatives in England. The British embassy in The Hague granted me a temporary visa for the United Kingdom.

Also, at that time, overseas flights couldn't land in Montreal; I had to fly via New York. So the American consulate in Amsterdam gave me a transit permit.

For the last few days in Holland, I went to visit the Brunns. On the last day I visited Shoshana, who was then in Amsterdam. I said good-bye to the three people who had been closest to me in Holland.

May 1, 1947. I left Amsterdam and flew to London in a small plane.

Even when I arrived in London, I had some difficulty. I was detained at Croydon airport by the British police.

My cousin was waiting for me while police held me back for over an hour. I don't know why—perhaps because I was travelling on an unusual document, or maybe they were checking my identity against lists of war criminals.

I had difficulty at every stop because of my irregular document. Fundamentally the problem was that I'd been born in Germany. This hampered me during the war—I could never admit to my birthplace—and now, even after the war, it was still tripping me up.

I was finally allowed to go through. I hadn't seen my relatives since 1937 when they had left their home in Dortmund, Germany.

Some days later I continued on my way. I took the train from London's Euston Station to Glasgow, Scotland. From Glasgow I went by bus to Prestwick where the flights for New York took off.

On the sixth of May, I flew from Prestwick to Iceland, from Iceland to Newfoundland, and from Newfoundland to New York. When I landed in New York, I was led aside. An epidemic of some sort had erupted in London and, since I'd come through there, I had to be inoculated.

I was hurried away to be given a needle. My brother stood waiting, bewildered when I didn't walk out!

Then I had to pass through Customs. I wasn't carrying much baggage, but I had to line up like everyone else.

Eddi saw me then. He sneaked in between the Customs Inspectors and came to my side. He was unbelievably happy!

An emotional moment seeing him again! I hadn't seen him for nine long years. We had last been together in 1938.

He looked very well—much better than I did. I had been on the road from London for about two days and I hadn't shaved. Eddi took me to a barbershop for a shave and a haircut. Then we boarded a plane to Montreal.

We arrived in Montreal and my travel document was stamped 'Landed Immigrant, Montreal Dorval Airport, May 7, 1947.'

CHAPTER XXV
EPILOGUE

In June of 1981, my late wife Leah and I flew to Europe. I wanted to show her the area where I was born and also the places and jails I had inhabited during the war.

Forty-three years after I had left my home town, Leah and I returned to Wattenscheid. We arrived by car and I couldn't recognize a thing. We parked the car and walked around, and gradually I picked out two landmarks—the Catholic and Evangelical churches. Then everything fell into place.

The coal mines are closed and, instead of slag heaps and grime, the streets are immaculately clean, the buildings freshly painted, the environment green and apparently free of pollution. Our home and main store are gone, leaving nothing in their place but a large empty lot: this becomes the outdoor market square one day a week and, at other times, provides parking for cars and bicycles for the adjoining business district which has become a pedestrian shopping mall. A tall new department store stands at the limit of what was once our property but the name emblazoned on the structure is not Hermann Schnitzer. Similarly, our former shoe store on the Oststrasse is tenanted now by a store with a different name. However, the large Woolworth store that was there when I was growing up is still there. And some of the buildings around the 'old market' square—our home—have been designated heritage sites. One of these is the Schulte Apotheke which still houses the pharmacy plus the office and home of Dr. Robert Schulte, my boyhood neighbor and friend.

Robert greeted us at his door with quick recognition and warmth and swept us into his home to meet and sit down with his family. He telephoned the Schrocks: Erwin had recently died—to my great regret—but Hedwig was still as sweet and good and beautiful as ever. She and another employee of my parents—a woman who had had a boyfriend in the SS—had saved pictures of my family and loaned them to us to make copies for me and Eddi. Hedwig told me of my mother's courage in venturing out of the Dortmund ghetto by covering the Jewish star with a fur neckpiece; my father's retention of his dignity by always being impeccably dressed; and Benno's tears and concern for my parents in spite of his own exhaustion.

From Bochum with its mixture of sad reminiscences, heart-warming encounters, an unanswerable undertone:

WHY? HOW COULD IT HAVE HAPPENED?

We visited several spas. Some, such as Bad Kreuznach, have essentially disappeared into the encroaching industrial area; others, such as Bad Neuenahr or Schlangenbad, are as pristine and perfect—and unreal—as they ever were.

We drove to Holland next and looked for the camp that had swallowed up my friends. Poorly-marked roads in a desolate region led eventually to a nature preserve frequented by happy cyclists and hikers. Buried within an unwholesome-looking vaporish swamp there is a simple unadorned memorial: a glass-enclosed case displays a model of Westerbork camp and a short piece of rail symbolizes the many transports that carried 100,000 Jews, mainly Dutch citizens, from there to Auschwitz and other death camps. The memorial was put up by a Jewish youth organization, not by the Dutch government. Perhaps the Dutch prefer not to draw attention to a camp which they themselves set up in 1938 to intern Jewish refugees from Germany and which the Nazi conquerors later took over ready-made for their diabolical purposes.

The town of Franeker was next on this odyssey. It's unchanged, picturesque and pretty. The old station building, site of the *hachshara*, has been modernized with new windows and doors and is now a private home. The van der Berg farm and the other farms I knew in the region are still operating family farms. And at the former Zuider Zee, the beautiful old sailing port of Hoorn maintains the island prison where I was jailed in 1940 by the Dutch and from which I was released a few days later, courtesy of the German army.

Amsterdam has almost obliterated its ancient Jewish quarter; Jewish life as it existed there in the 1930's has disappeared. The magnificent historical structure of the Portuguese synagogue is a solitary relic. As in so many other European cities, the streets of Amsterdam are essentially *Judenrein* (free of Jews).

A Swiss colleague, Jean Neyroud, tried to unearth the document I was forced to sign in 1942 which ordered my expulsion from Switzerland, but he was told that such documents had all been destroyed. Were they destroyed?—or are the Swiss authorities reluctant to publicize what they did during the war years? The question nags me especially since my colleague was warned that I could be arrested even now if I returned to Switzerland because I had entered illegally in 1942. I returned to Switzerland nevertheless, in 1981 at the invitation of the Chemical Society of Bern and later at the request of Swiss television to recount my wartime experiences. In La-Chaux-de-Fonds we quickly spotted the ineradicable image, the cantonal jail, though it has been enlarged with a new wing since the fateful day I spent there in 1942.

From La Chaux-de-Fonds we drove toward the Doubs River in heavy rain and mist. The road is narrow and sparsely travelled with steep cliffs on both sides of the river which flows violently. The whole area is thickly wooded and not much developed to this day. Where one crosses into France at Fournet Blancheroche, the church in the little village square still dominates the heights and I silently recalled the old priest who thought that Piefke and I were angels.

At Besançon we visited the cathedral and the Archbishop's palace. Then, after careful perusal of a city map, we found the awesome prison fronting on a deceptively quiet road. In Arbois, too—the town of Louis Pasteur—we located the church, now a museum, and, close by, the quiet street flanked by a high jail wall.

In Dijon we visited the railway station from which I was shipped as a prisoner to Belgium. In Brussels we tramped through much of the city, including the seedy area near the Gare du Nord and along the Rue Verte, which is still a red light district. The prison at St. Gilles, which we didn't revisit, was reportedly still functioning. And Waterloo has become a busy suburb of Brussels; Fernand's farm is no longer there.

Then we drove to Fexhe-le-Haut-Clocher. It's still isolated: the main highway passes a few kilometres north of it. We easily found the Roberti farm but it was no longer in use. The buildings were deserted and run down, windows were broken, and weeds were growing in the farmyard. An old caretaker told us that the farm was to be put up for auction for a housing development.

Curiosity finally took us to Wavre. It proved to be a busy industrial city south of Brussels. In the main square stands an eloquent memorial to the martyrs of the resistance: obviously the citizenry had been active in fighting the Nazi occupation. Since my Belgian identity card was issued in Wavre, we checked the city map in the display case outside the city hall; and, yes, there is a Chaussée de Bruxelles. In the telephone directory, we found several listings for the name Van Capelle. Coincidence? Or a miracle? Was my passion for football so trivial after all?—it gave me Jan Van Capelle and, with him, guardian angels in the city of Wavre, Dirk the painter, and last but certainly not least, the old farmer Monsieur Degive.

P.S. In March of 1999, after 25 years of repeated enquiries, my Swiss colleague, Jean Neyroud, managed to secure an extract of the 1942 record from the prison of La Chaux-de-Fonds. It stated that M. Schnitzer, prisoner No. 249, a person of the Jewish religion, was returned to the French border on August 28, 1942. Thus, 57 years after throwing me to the Germans, the Swiss police confirmed this event—without an apology...

INDEX